A.

The Road Taken

A Memoir

By

Ann Garratt

This edition published 2015 by
Bunlacky Press
Castletown
Dunkineely
County Donegal
Ireland

First published in paperback in 2014 by CreateSpace
Independent Publishing Platform
Kindle version published 2014

ISBN: 978-0-9931784-0-5

I wish to thank my husband, Charlie, for his help and encouragement in writing this memoir, my daughters, Marianne and Jenny, for their insightful comments, and my brothers and sisters for digging deep into their past to assist me. Special thanks to the Mountcharles writing group without whom this work would not have been completed. Alison Walsh was a supportive and discerning editor, guiding me through from rough draft to final version.

Contents

Preface - Regrouping

I'm just an ordinary person, but an extraordinary event in my life set me on the path to writing this memoir. It began in November 1993, when I suffered from paranoid delusions. I became convinced that I was being followed by white cars and spied on by airplanes. As I recovered and began to look for answers, I found that my story was not just about mental illness, but also one of emigration, family, and the search for identity.

In 1995, whilst I was still living in Warwickshire, my husband Charlie and I bought a holiday home in Donegal, where I spent my early years. Being 'home' triggered long-forgotten incidents and emotions. I met relatives I hadn't seen for years and old friends of my parents, who recounted fond memories of them. Being in Ireland, walking the lanes, inhaling the damp, turf-laden air, triggered recollections, and each time I returned to England, where I had lived from the age of seven, I found I brought with me more of my Irish identity, a part of me that had slipped away over the years.

When I moved back to Donegal permanently in 2006, I had time on my hands. I had always nursed an ambition to write. Then I joined a writers' group, I began producing short pieces about my childhood and was flabbergasted when they were broadcast by RTE as part of their "Quiet Corner" in 2010. It was also around this time that I read Flora Thompson's excellent memoir of rural life, *Lark Rise to Candleford*. By the time she came to write about her life in Oxfordshire, the world she described had all but vanished. Similarly, the world I found when I emigrated to Coventry in 1959 and the Ireland I remembered of the fifties had also disappeared. I felt a need to chronicle those times, before all traces were gone. And so, I began. Week by week, the 2,000 words I had produced for the radio programme were added to and embellished.

My journey into my past was not always an easy one. Troubling memories were unearthed and long-buried emotions came to the fore. Unexpectedly, confusion over my national and cultural identity became a central theme of my story. What started out as a few short pieces on moving away from Ireland developed into a much deeper examination of who I am and where I feel I belong. Memory is a strange thing and often plays tricks on us. Given the wet and windy climate of Donegal why is it most of my childhood memories there, are framed warm sunny days? Family stories are told and retold and bend and alter with the retelling and although I have tried hard to accurately represent my childhood, sometimes those recollections don't always tally with those of my siblings. As a consequence, when I came to write about my life I tried to separate family myth from memory, but when I struggled to know the difference, my guiding principle was: am I being true to myself and what I believe to be true?

Finally because of the sensitive nature of some aspects of my story I have changed the names of certain individuals.

My childhood was sometimes difficult and challenging, but on the whole it was a happy one. I could have fictionalised the account of my past, but in the end I decided I needed to own it, to say honestly to the world, this is my story.

Chapter 1 - Crisis

The process of writing this memoir began in 2006, but my journey towards it started twelve years earlier, with a difficult and painful mental illness, which reached crisis point one dark evening in February 1994.

Neon lights flashed high above me as music blared from the shops onto the busy London street. Crowds of people surged around me, dodging each other on their way to the Tube station. I stood for a moment trembling, trying to concentrate. Was the music thumping out a secret message to me? I listened again, hoping to catch the words. They meant nothing. I turned my attention to the passing traffic. No white cars and the number plates were too random to mean anything. I was safe, for now. For months, I had been convinced that the government was sending out secret messages to me via the radio and TV and it had a fleet cars assigned to follow me, tracking my every move. I believed I was being spied on by everyone around me and I rarely went out, preferring the cover of darkness when I felt safest.

At a wig stand in a department store, I bought a curly auburn wig and rushed to the loo to put it on. Outside again, I darted round and round Piccadilly Circus, trying to throw "them" off. When I was sure no-one was following me, I made my way back to the car, unlocked the door and climbed onto the leather seat. It felt comforting, familiar, like home.

Starting up the engine, I had no sense of where I was headed. I had an idea that I could sleep overnight in the car and then maybe travel to France in the morning, where I hoped to become invisible. It was growing dark, the street lamps were casting shadows on the road, the headlights of the cars coming towards me were making me feel dizzy. I thought about my husband, Charlie, and my girls, Marianne and Jenny. They'd be frantic. Stopping at a phone booth, my heart pounding, I dialled my home number. As I heard my husband's voice I burst into tears. His pain and frustration were evident as he pleaded with me to come home. I hesitated. I had thought that by running away I'd escape my demons but now I realised that I loved my family too much to cause them more grief. I climbed into my car and headed through the enveloping darkness a hundred miles back up the motorway to home.

A week later I sat, quivering, in a tiny windowless office and blurted out my story to a rosy-faced psychiatrist. He didn't look in the least surprised and smiled encouragingly at me. "Are you a hundred per cent sure that what you're telling me is real? That you are being followed and there is some kind of conspiracy against you?"

I thought for a moment. It was a difficult one. "No. I'm not totally convinced, but maybe about eighty-five per cent," I said.

He stared at me for a second, as if trying to decide something, and then he smiled reassuringly. "I think I can help." He explained that because I wasn't one hundred per cent convinced by my delusions, I had retained some insight and thus, although my symptoms were alarming, they were evidence that I was suffering from severe depression rather than something more extreme, like schizophrenia or bi-polar disorder. I could be treated with anti-depressants but, in the meantime, he gave me some anti-psychotic drugs to help clear up my delusions. I was so relieved to get the diagnosis: At last somebody had taken notice of my condition and given me hope that I might get well again. Amazingly, within a week, the feelings of paranoia started to fade. I was on the road to recovery, but still a long way from feeling well again.

My problems had begun in the autumn of 1993 when I had a senior job in the NHS and was within the top five per cent of female earners in the country. By anyone's standards, I had a successful career. I was responsible for a budget of £30 million plus and my job was commissioning mental health services for half the population of Birmingham; this involved the planning of psychiatric hospitals and community-based services, monitoring the quality of care provided and initiating new developments. Most of my days were taken up with wall-to-wall meetings and with the responsibility of making decisions that affected thousands of people.

I had been on a lovely holiday to France and returned to find myself in the midst of a further re-organisation at work. We had already been through one major one, which saw the number of health authorities in Birmingham shrink from five to two. Our chief executive had been sacked and there was talk of large-scale redundancies. Everyone was under a great deal of pressure and the whole atmosphere was one of distrust and suspicion. Out of the blue, I started to experience strong feelings of fear and apprehension and that was when I became convinced that my office was bugged and that I was being followed around the city by a fleet of cars. I grew more and more fearful and isolated until I just ground to a halt. I knew I couldn't bear to continue, and after a lot of soul-searching, decided to hand in my notice. Exhausted, I needed a break. The anti-depressants prescribed by my GP made no difference. If anything, I was getting worse. I was convinced the telephone and house were under surveillance. My state of mind was such that I even thought I was responsible for the weather. Over the following two years, I was referred to numerous counsellors. They listened with patience, and suggested rest and relaxation. I didn't know where to turn. Although I was receiving help, it wasn't working. I was still certain I was at the centre of an enormous government conspiracy.

On reflection, my nightmare seemed to stem from a period a few years earlier when I had worked for a drugs and alcohol charity. I was a development officer based at the regional office, which ran a number of drug projects all around the West Midlands. It was a Saturday and I had woken to the sound of the phone ringing downstairs. Peter, my boss, was on the line. He was distraught.

"Lisa has been murdered. I've just spent the night in a police cell. They think it was me." My heart started to pound and I could feel the blood rushing to my head. "Are you sure it wasn't suicide" I suggested.

"She has been beaten to death in the project. It happened yesterday when I had an appointment to see her. They let me go an hour ago," Peter said.

I couldn't believe what I was hearing. Lisa was someone I worked with, an ex-drug-user, a beautiful, talented young woman. She was full of mischief and laughter. That she'd been murdered just as she was getting her life back together seemed horribly ironic. Over the next few weeks work went crazy. The papers screamed headlines of "Angel of Mercy murdered" and "Charity worker slain." I was right in the thick of it. Peter was eventually eliminated from the investigation, but then I heard that Darren, Lisa's boss, was being held. A few days later, he was charged with her murder. I was dumbfounded and felt terrible. I had known Darren for several years and had even suggested him for the job. I liked and respected him. To my horror, I realised that if it hadn't been for me, they would never have met and Lisa would still be alive. A sympathetic policeman remarked to me that it was very unusual to know both the murderer and victim. He said it must be difficult to deal with, and so it was. Most upsetting was the fact that Lisa had approached me a few months earlier saying she had concerns about Darren and his commitment to work. He wasn't doing his fair share. Lisa went on sick leave and I passed my concerns onto Peter.

For some months the project had been under an internal investigation following the discovery of some financial irregularities. In hindsight, this seemed to crank up the tension. On the day Lisa was killed Peter had come to meet her to discuss the financial shortfall. The courts found that

Darren had probably murdered her when she threatened to expose him as a thief: the police investigation revealed Darren had been embezzling large amounts of cash from work to pay his mortgage. I had suggested he was a bad manager, but had never in my wildest dreams imagined that his behaviour could have escalated in the way it did.

The police investigation was bad enough, but the internal enquiry afterwards was even more horrendous. Work papers, minutes of meetings, supervision notes were all scrutinised by a team from head office. It was clear that they wanted to point the finger at someone. When they got round to checking Darren's references, I heaved a huge sigh of relief when it turned out they were genuine.

I felt so shaken by the whole episode, that after fifteen years' absence, I started going to church again, in the hope that religion could offer some solace. Most of all, I struggled to understand how Darren, a person I had known and admired, could be responsible for such a malevolent act. It made me question my belief in myself and in my judgement. Time and time again I asked myself, how could I have been so wrong about him? The sense of confusion and shock arising from this whole episode was to haunt me for many years after the event and the anxiety I endured in coming to terms with it was, I guess, one of the triggers to the onset of my mental health problems.

In 1994, when I resigned from my NHS post, I decided to become self-employed. I didn't feel able to hold down a job and the option of self-employment seemed to allow me greater flexibility. Jobs came in fits and starts and I could get on with them at my own pace. The pressure started to lift.

In the early nineties, Charlie and I took a break in Ireland, firstly to Galway and then to Donegal. For me it represented an opportunity to revisit my roots, to rekindle my Irish heritage. At a time when I was questioning everything about myself, Ireland seemed to offer some respite. It was quiet and I found I could relax. The gentle pace of life and the friendliness of the people represented something that was absent from my life. I was smitten and after several summers spent in Donegal, I eventually persuaded Charlie that we should look for a holiday home there.

At that time, property in Donegal was very cheap and although our budget was small, there were plenty of small cottages on offer. I was keen to try and get something near my mother's old family home, but found that for the most part, houses in that neck of the woods were out of our price range. So instead, we concentrated on the area around Donegal Town.

At the end of one long day of fruitless searching, the estate agent remarked that he had one more place to show us. "It's thatched. A bit dilapidated, but it's a lovely wee house. I grew up in a cottage just like it."

Charlie and I looked at each other. We felt sorry for him: he seemed desperate to make a sale, so reluctantly, we agreed to take a look. It was lashing down and we peered out through the windscreen wipers at a tiny, white cottage with a black door, sitting forlornly by the edge of a road. It looked neglected: the white paint was rusted with soot on the outside walls and the thatch was beginning to collapse. But it had charm. We decided to venture inside. It smelled damp and musty. There were just three rooms, a living room, bedroom and bathroom. There was dirt and dust everywhere, a feeble old range dominated the main room and a battered settee languished along one wall. It would need to be completely renovated and extended, but I fell in love with it immediately. It reminded me of my granny's in Loughfad. We paid the deposit that day.

Charlie often says the decision to buy a home in Donegal was one of the best we ever made, even though it was at a time when I was still unwell and suffering from paranoid delusions. To me, the cottage represented a bolt hole, somewhere to go to escape from the world which was threatening to engulf me. We threw ourselves into the business of renovating and extending it. By mid-1995, our work was complete and we were the proud owners of a traditional, cosy, country residence in Castletown, a townland about eight miles from Donegal Town.

We knew nothing of the area but found two great neighbours. On one side was Cassie Meehan, a woman in her eighties, and on the other, Bella Kilday, a lovely lady who had never married and lived on her own in a tumbledown stone cottage. Bella and Cassie introduced us to the neighbourhood and advised on where to shop, what to buy and who to meet. Charlie plays guitar and found there was a traditional music session in a bar in the town every Wednesday night. We adored everything about our new home and the kind and generous people around the town who became our friends. Sometimes, when the rain and the wind swirled noisily around us, we didn't even venture out, but sat curled up by the fire reading and listening to the radio. Bliss.

Gradually, as I began to recover, I felt that our little cottage was in some way responsible. It seemed to me at the time that Ireland was paying me back, making restitution for letting me go all those years ago. I was rediscovering everything I'd left behind, the deserted beaches and the unforgettable perfume of the turf fires carried in the wind. Charlie loved the place, too. For him, it represented a chance to escape from the constant drone of the motorway, cramped railway carriages and the pressure of work.

When one experiences a serious mental health problem as I did, there is a need to try and understand why. I accepted that in my work I was under a lot of strain, but lots of people under similar pressures don't go on to develop mental health problems. So I asked myself, why me? I didn't have a history of mental illness, and although my mother suffered from depression, no-one in the family had suffered the kind of breakdown I'd experienced.

As I began to put my life back together, I read dozens of books on the subject and trawled the internet looking for an answer. I found the statistic that the Irish in the UK are twice as likely to be admitted to psychiatric hospitals as the native population and to suffer high rates of depression and suicide. In addition, the incidence of psychosis is often associated with arriving in England before the age of eleven. Now, I wondered if this related to me.

No-one knows for sure the reasons for this shocking fact, but isolation and poverty are likely culprits. I think back to my own childhood when we first arrived in Coventry, when, sometimes, I was overwhelmed by feelings of loss and uncertainty. Maybe one of the factors behind my breakdown had been my emigration to England as a child. I thought of my mother, with her ongoing depression, and of my father and his dark moods. Were they, too, casualties of immigration? I didn't know. But in some ways, I felt relieved. It pointed the finger away from me as an individual and to the wider picture, one I shared with thousands of other Irish emigrants. It seemed to me the answers I was looking for might have their roots in my past, and that to understand more about myself, I would need to look backwards, to that first uprooting from my home in Falcarragh, Co. Donegal, as my family searched for a better life in a new country.

Chapter 2 - A Noisy Bustle

My emigrant story begins in 1959, amid the bustle of a train station, a theatre of steam rising, whistles blowing, Tannoy screeching, brakes screaming, porters pointing and passengers scurrying to make their connections. I was seven years old. I'd never seen a train before, and I was awestruck. We had caught the train in Strabane in Northern Ireland and were on our way to the port of Belfast.

I was so excited I couldn't hold back. "Is this Coventry, Mammy? Have we arrived?" I asked.

"No, Ann, we have to go on a big boat yet. Don't be impatient. We'll arrive in Coventry soon enough, you'll see," Mammy answered.

The locomotive drew in and we all clambered out. We gazed around. Most people seemed to know where they were going but a few, like us, stood transfixed as they struggled to make sense of the bustling station. There were dozens of adults staggering along, wearing long heavy coats, hats pulled down over their ears, awkwardly balancing bulging cases on each arm, trailed by their offspring. They looked troubled, uncertain, anxious.

"Keep close to your daddy," Mammy was clutching Michael, the baby, in her arms and had Charlie, my brother, who was three, by the hand. My other two brothers Pat, Johnjoe and I trailed after Daddy, who was loaded down with luggage.

"Watch the boys, Ann, make sure no-one gets lost," Mammy ordered.

I already had hold of each of my younger brothers by the hand, but I tightened my grip. We were heading for the exit. I wanted to stop and stare; I didn't want to miss anything. Coming from a small town in rural Donegal, I'd never seen so many people in my entire life. I was curious about them. I wanted to know who they were, what they were doing here; if they were for the boat like us.

"Ann, will you hurry on or we're going to miss that ferry," Daddy scolded.

"Everyone keep together," said Mammy.

"I'm hungry, I want my tea," Pat wailed.

Mammy stroked his head. "We haven't time, Pat, we'll have something later, but now we need to get going, otherwise we'll never make it."

Johnjoe, who was only four, was complaining, "I want to go home. I don't like it here." He was covering his ears with his hands to drown out the noise.

I crouched down beside him. "We're going on a big boat. You'll like that. You like boats."

That seemed to reassure him and he smiled.

"Then can we go home?" he said.

In no time at all we were outside, speeding through Belfast in a taxi, the old tram lines criss-crossing the roads in front of us. Through the taxi window, the evening city flickered past. People were hurrying along eager to make their way home from work, young men and women were dodging in and out of the traffic on bicycles. The buses were overloaded with tired bodies, pushing and shoving to claim a seat. It was like a newsreel, crowds everywhere, rushing, heads down, wrapped in gabardine raincoats. By the time we reached the dock, daylight had given way to darkness. We couldn't see very much, just an enormous gangway leading up to the ferry. Daddy pulled out our tickets and we climbed up the steps to the boat. Once inside, we were directed to the berths below deck. Down and down we went into the bowels of the ship. Below, the corridors were jammed with people and suitcases; children were crying and men and women were shouting across to one another.

Daddy was first to find our cabin and we all filed in, tired but content to shut the door on all the noise and chaos outside.

Inside, a row erupted. Pat and I were fighting over who could have the top bunk. We had never seen bunk beds before and we both wanted the top one, because it had a port hole. You could just about make out what was going on in the decks outside.

"Mammy, can I have it?" I pleaded. "I'm older than him. He might fall when he's asleep."

"That's not fair," Pat protested. "She always gets her own way. I think I should have the top. I won't fall out, I know I won't."

"Yes, you will, you'll fall and hurt yourself, and cry and wake everybody up."

"I won't. Only babies cry."

"Yes you will. You'll be bawling like a baby."

Finally, Mammy barked, "Cease your arguing at once. I'm sick of having to tell you both to stop fighting. It's been a long day and we're all tired. God knows it's a tight squeeze in here and there's no room for arguments. You can both have the top bunk. Ann at the head and Pat at the bottom. I'll not hear another word from either of you."

Pat and I stared angrily at each other, but it was settled. We knew not to question our mother any further: we didn't dare. We had each got what we wanted, the top bunk, but I had the port hole. I climbed up and peered out. The docks were lit up, and under the lamp posts I could see people standing by the quayside, waving goodbye to friends and family. Suddenly the engine started. It made such a loud noise and the boat vibrated. I felt a shudder of fright. Were we sinking? No, we were moving. I glanced through my porthole into the moonlit navy blue night. The boat was slipping away from the quayside into the darkness.

"I'm still hungry," Pat moaned.

"Well you've had your tea, there's nothing now till morning," Mammy said.

Just then Daddy put his jacket on. "I'm just going for a turn around the boat. Give us a few bob."

Mammy groaned and reached for her purse. "Here, that's all I have. Don't be long. Not tonight, James, when we've this big journey ahead of us and I have to settle the wains."

Daddy smiled as Mammy dropped a few coins into his hand. "Just the one then." He saluted her and was swiftly out of the door.

Mammy threw her eyes heavenward and fished out a bottle from her bag and started to feed Michael. Pat and I took Charlie and Johnjoe to the toilet and then helped get them ready for bed. They were tired and cranky after the long day. We tucked their little bodies into the bunks, gave them dummies and in two minutes they were sound asleep. Satisfied, I climbed up the ladder to my bunk again. Pat was already there, peering out of the porthole.

"I can see matchstick men walking about on the shore; they're getting smaller and smaller. Soon they'll disappear and we will be on our own alone at sea."

"They'll be lots of other boats. Isn't that true Mammy," I declared.

"That's right, Ann," Mammy reassured us. Then she added, "Right you two, down under the blankets."

Reluctantly Pat moved to the bottom. We both climbed beneath the sheets.

"By this time tomorrow, we'll be in Coventry. It's a lot different to what you've been used to. It's the big city," Mammy said.

Pat stopped his wriggling for a minute. "Is everyone on the boat going to Coventry, Mammy?"

"No, they'll be going to Birmingham and London - all over the place. England's a huge country. Only the very lucky ones will be going to Coventry. There are parks to play in, shops galore and huge double-decker buses."

"What's a double-decker bus?" Pat asked.

"You'll see when you get there. There's lots to do and new friends to make. We can all make new friends. Even your daddy can make new friends. Ones that don't keep him in the pub all night. What do you say to that?"

Mammy reached up for her goodnight kiss and I wrapped my arms around her.

"When I wake, will we be there?"

"Nearly."

My heart was bursting with anticipation as I snuggled down under the bedclothes and could feel Pat's feet tickling mine. In another second, though, he stopped wriggling and sat bolt upright.

"If a powerful wind comes then we could get shipwrecked, we'd all drown and we'll never get to England."

"Oh, caddie, stop exaggerating. Of course we won't sink. This is a massive boat, it won't sink even if the weather's bad," Mammy reassured him.

I smiled to myself. Like all boys, Pat loved to imagine the worst.

I had been asleep for ages, when I woke to find Daddy shouting.

"Nora? Nora, is that you? Where the devil are you?"

The lights went on and Michael started to cry. "Whisht now, it's only your daddy. For the love of God, James. What time do you call this? You're drunk. And this of all nights," Mammy said.

Daddy was still trying to find his berth.

"You're under me, Daddy. You're sleeping under me," I whispered loudly, trying not to disturb the others.

"Ah, Ann, I knew I could rely on you. Come on, give your daddy a big hug before he settles down for the night."

Daddy wrapped his arms tightly around me. His breath smelled of drink and he bent close to my ears, his voice little more than a whisper. "Never forget where you're from. Ireland's the place you were born. Where you were reared. There's no place like it on Earth. Ha, ha, the ol' country, God's Own Country." You're an Irish girl. Be proud of that always. Promise me you will."

"I promise, Daddy."

"You're a grand girl, Ann. I know you'll never forget and I'm sure wherever we end up, it will always be alive in my heart." He straightened up, struggling to compose himself.

Mammy was in no mood for his drunken ramblings. "Jesus, Mary and Joseph. What are you blathering about? Stop acting the goat and leave the child alone. Get to your bed."

He stumbled into his berth, mumbling softly to himself. In a moment, I could hear him snoring.

Mammy put the lights out and the cabin was once again in darkness. The boat was humming softly. I looked out of my porthole. It was very dark outside, I couldn't see anything. I thought of my friends tucked up in bed in Donegal. Wouldn't they envy me now, here on a boat sailing away to a new life? I couldn't wait for morning.

Chapter 3 - Home by the Sea

That night on the boat was another stepping stone in my journey from Falcarragh, a small town resting quietly on the stunning north coast of Donegal. Pink, lemon and green houses jostled for space on the main street, interspersed by a church, shops, a garage, pubs and a hardware store. We even had an ice-cream parlour. Nearly everything we wished for could be bought locally and for anything else we relied on the town fair, which was held once a week.

For her vegetables my mother walked to a walled garden at the far end of the town. Bees were also kept there and, for a few coppers, we enjoyed the delights of fresh honey straight from the honeycomb. At the bottom end of Falcarragh, the church towered above the few scattered houses and the school building stood opposite by the roadside. There were several pubs, each with dusky interiors, where, at any time of the day, men could be found in corners crouched over their beer, enjoying the craic.

Bounded on one side by the Atlantic Sea and the navy dappled screed of the Derryveagh Mountains on the other, Falcarragh seemed like a frontier town tucked in at the end of the world. From our kitchen window, we could see the flat top of Muckish Mountain standing guard over our small settlement.

Overall, there was nothing exceptional about the place: such villages were to be found up and down the country but with its magnificent setting, we thought it was blessed, a town like no other in Ireland. The area was and is well known for its white sandy beaches and often, during the summer, Mammy would take us to the beach. Screaming with shouts of joy, Pat and I would tumble down the sand dunes and then create elaborate sandcastles, only to see them eventually washed away by the tides. We loved to paddle in the waves and go for long walks along the water's edge, stopping from time to time, watching the tiny sea creatures in the rock pools and collecting small crabs in our buckets.

This idyllic time ended when, at four, I was sent to nursery school in Ballyconnell House, with the nuns. It was the first time I'd spied a nun and I screamed in terror: with their long black robes and white faces, they seemed like huge crows bearing down on me. I refused to go inside and had to be dragged across the threshold. Someone gave me a biscuit and I threw it down in disgust. My mother was humiliated. She slapped me round the legs and left me to their mercy. I roared and cried, great tears rolling down my face. I was inconsolable but it made no difference. They kept me there.

Things didn't improve. I loathed the place. Every day I begged my mammy not to take me. I would lie down on the street having tantrums all the way. At break times, the older children would hang around in the toilets and pull my knickers down. After this happened to me a few times, I used to wet myself rather than go to the toilet. I never told anyone; I was too ashamed.

Life improved greatly when I left Ballyconnell and joined the national school at the far end of the town. In contrast to my previous experience, the children here were good to me, I wasn't bullied and for the first time, my lessons seemed like fun. Even though we didn't speak Irish at home, I found I enjoyed the experience of learning new Irish words and couldn't wait to test them out on Mammy when I got home. I soon made friends and each night I walked home from school with a gang of girls my own age. At school, we learned about Brian Boru, St Patrick and the bloody history of the establishment of the Free State. The fierce struggle for independence that had been waged by brave Irishmen captured my imagination and I was filled with pride for my young country.

On alternate Fridays, we were given a loaf of bread or a packet of hot chocolate to take home. The loaf was fresh and soft in the middle, with a tasty hard crust outside. By the time

I got home, either the inside of the bread was plucked clean or my mouth would be covered with delicious chocolate powder.

Looking back on those days, there's a childish impression that the sun always shone, but in truth, for much of the time, a cold, harsh wind bustled through the streets as people, hugging their coats about them, made their way from one end of the town to the other. There was a hardiness about the inhabitants who had a readiness to engage with life and the elements. People were not about to be beaten and there was an excitement and vibrancy about the place.

Although there was hardship in the town, with many of the men working away in Scotland, I sensed that my parents and their friends felt optimistic that things would improve. Several new businesses were starting up. My father's friend, John Kelly, opened a hardware store, my mother's friends, the McGees, opened a garage and my daddy invested in a picture house with his cousin.

We were proud citizens of a young country. Barely thirty-five years had passed since independence and every person on every street corner had an opinion about how to run it. Talk of de Valera and local politicians was much on the lips of the adults around me. I listened, open-mouthed, as they were cursed and praised in equal measure. The national flag was boldly displayed on homes and businesses up and down the town and I loved its soft green and gold colours.

By the time I'd settled at the national school, our family had grown. First was Pat, a couple of years younger than me, who was born at Letterkenny Hospital. Dad and I picked him and Mammy up in the van, carefully placing him in the back in his Moses basket whilst the three of us sat in the front. My dad was so nervous that every few miles he kept stopping to make sure the baby was okay. Pat slept soundly the whole time, only stirring when Dad poked him to make sure he was still alive.

Johnjoe was born a year later. A big baby, he weighed over twelve pounds. My mother always maintained he was so strong he could sit up right away. This early development was not characteristic of the rest of his first years, as he was well over three when he said his first words. Mum was so concerned, she sent him to the doctor's, to no avail. Months went by and still not a peep from Johnjoe. Then, one day, he looked up at her and uttered, "See the lovely wee flowers, Mammy." She couldn't believe it. Johnjoe had clearly been saving his words up for a sentence. She was overjoyed.

Charlie, my third brother, was born at home. Many years later, Mammy told me how my dad went out anxiously to fetch the doctor when her pains started. It took all of Dad's powers of persuasion to get him there, because the baby wasn't due for some weeks. When they finally reached our house, it was to find my mum in the process of giving birth.

"The baby's being born, Doctor," Mammy cried out in distress, as they all rushed round with towels and blankets. The labour had taken just over an hour and Charlie was her only child to be delivered normally: all the rest were caesarean births.

The last of our family to be born in Ireland, Michael, was delivered in Dungloe hospital. Again, he was a big baby, over ten pounds in weight. When I first saw him, I thought he was like a little monkey with his huge eyes and a very long, bendy body. I adored all the babies. They were like live dolls, much better than one bought at a shop. They laughed when I tickled them, and didn't seem to mind when I dressed them up in my dollies' clothes.

After having five children in seven years, my poor mother was exhausted. No wonder she sent me off to the nuns for some respite. Also, from time to time, my brothers often stayed with relatives to give mammy a rest. My father's cousin had no children of her own at the time and often helped out.

She regularly took Johnjoe and Charlie to stay overnight. She was particularly fond of Charlie, which was not surprising, for he was an adorable child, with light blue eyes and a head full of blond curls.

We weren't the only ones with a large family and in those days, it wasn't unknown for childless relatives to raise their nieces and nephews. One of my father's sisters, Kay, was reared by an aunt. I only recently discovered that she was a full sister to my father. I had always been told she was a half-sister. I can only guess that my father had felt ashamed that his sister had been given away and only told us a half-truth. Whatever the reason, financial or otherwise, I was told the family put out the story that help was needed on the farm. Apparently at first it had been suggested my father go, however, he cried and lamented so much at the prospect, that his parents relented and sent his sister instead.

Being farmed out was almost my fate too. When I was eight or nine, my father's half-sister Rose and her husband, who were childless, came from America to visit us in Coventry. (My father had a half-brother and -sister, Rose and Patrick, his mother's children by her first husband, who had died.) Throughout their visit, I acted as their guide, and we became quite close. Before they were due to return home, they approached my mother and asked if they could take me back to live with them. They reassured her that they'd make a good home for me and that I wouldn't want for anything.

My mother didn't know what to say, and replied that she would have to ask me. Later she spoke quietly to me. "They're well off. This could be a great opportunity for you, Ann. Would you like to go?"

I was fond of them and flattered that they should want me, but I couldn't bear to be parted from my family so I declined the offer. I never regretted it.

One of the most enduring memories I have of Falcarragh was of the day the circus came to town. I must have been about five or six at the time. It was during the school holidays, in the middle of a hot and dusty summer. On the morning in question, I was bored and frustrated, having been told off yet again for arguing and fighting with my brother, Pat. I was sitting sulking, entertaining myself by finding faces in the squiggly patterns of the living-room curtains, when there was a rumbling noise outside. As I glanced out of the window I couldn't believe my eyes: an elephant was staring in at me. I opened my mouth to call my brother, but before I could utter a syllable, my mother shrieked loudly from the bedroom upstairs., 'Jesus, Mary and Joseph, what do you think you're doing?"

She was talking to the keeper, who was standing beside the elephant, calmly letting him nibble the grass in our front garden. Mammy shouted again, "Get that elephant out of here, he's ruining the lawn."

For my part, I was captivated and enchanted. Amazed that something I had only ever seen in books could actually be here in my garden. In my very own garden. It was a dark grey colour, its legs all wrinkly the size of tree trunks, and nearly half the size of our house.

Anxious not to offend us any further, the man muttered, "Sorry Missus", bowed apologetically and led the elephant on up the street.

"Can't we keep it, Mammy?" I said.

"No, Ann, it belongs in the circus. But if you're a good girl, we can go along and see it later tonight."

This was the most exciting thing that had ever happened to me in my life, except for the day we got Pat from the hospital. I couldn't wait to find Marie, a friend from school, and tell her about the circus, she'd be sure to be interested. She'll never believe I had an elephant in my garden, I thought. It was a clear bright day, the sun high in the sky. The yellow and pink houses on the street glistened in the sunlight; they looked clean, fresh. I shaded my eyes and saw a long parade of people from the circus passing by.

They were dressed in costumes of shimmering reds, greens, and blues. Horses' hooves were clattering on the roadside, drums were banging, people chanted and clapped. I stood, spellbound, at my front door as one by one they marched on and up into the town.

"Can I follow them up the street, Mammy?"

"All right," she agreed, "but stay well away from the horses: they look as if they should be in the wild west, not here in Falcarragh."

I chased the parade up the road, past familiar houses, the hardware store, and garage, to Marie's house. I knocked on the door. "Can Marie come out to play, the circus is here," I said, unable to contain my excitement.

Marie's mammy turned and shouted over her shoulder, "Marie, it's Ann, she wants you to come and see the circus, it's just coming up the street."

Marie then emerged from the house, eating a sandwich, jam all round her mouth.

"Now, be careful you two and calm down. Stand here at the door and it will go past. You'll see everything," her mother ordered.

At that moment two women in swimming costumes decorated with feathers, passed, holding a banner aloft, proclaiming the arrival of the circus.

"There's been an elephant in our garden. Mammy chased it. We're going there tonight. They have lions as well as elephants," I yelled.

The women were followed by a band of boy drummers who left us with the sound of drums ringing in our ears. Next came the horses. Frisky and eager to reach their destination, they surged forward, dressed in fancy ribbons, ridden by girls whose costumes shimmered and sparkled in the morning sun. A man was walking on stilts, poised precariously. He stretched down and handed leaflets to Marie and me.

"Get your mammy and daddy to bring you to the circus, it's a once-in-a-lifetime opportunity; they'll never see anything quite like this again."

"Mammy says we can come tonight."

"There's a good girl,' he said. "Have a balloon and tell all your friends."

Dozens of clowns were running around presenting more balloons to the children clambering around the parade. There was the tinkling of excited laughter as each child fought his or her way through to claim one. We stood holding ours as eventually the elephants and their keepers strode into view. With powerful legs marching in time to the beat of the drums, the huge beasts towered above everyone else in the procession. Although they were enormous, they seemed like gentle creatures; they had such soft friendly eyes. I wondered what it would feel like to stroke one, I supposed it would be all leathery, like an old pair of shoes. The lions came last, safely enclosed in an iron cage on the back of a lorry. They stood restlessly surveying their audience, snarling, looking menacing. As if they could, with one strike of their paw, slice you open. I shivered in fright.

"Did you see that, a real lion. It snarled at me. It's a good thing it's locked up. I bet it could eat somebody up in one bite. maybe it would eat up Mrs McGinty,' Marie said. Our teacher was very strict and we were all scared of her.

"How could you be saying such a thing, Marie. You're a wicked girl, don't let me hear you speaking like that again,"

Marie's mammy scolded but she had a grin on her face.

For a moment I had an image of the lion jumping down from the cage, grabbing Mrs McGinty in his jaws and running up Muckish Mountain. Maybe then we wouldn't have to do Irish in class. That was an appealing idea.

As quickly as it had arrived, the circus disappeared away up the road.

"Well, that's that," Marie's mammy proclaimed and went back into the house. We were left standing outside, feeling a little disappointed now all the excitement had passed.

"Shall we follow them?" I heard myself say to Marie.

"Mammy says they're going to a field past the church at the far end of the town, it's just by the school."

"I don't think my mammy will let me," Marie said. "She'd be cross."

"She won't know," I argued. "We'll be back before she misses us."

Now we ran on, following the circus, over the crossroads at the middle of town and caught it up just as it passed our school and came to a stop outside the field. Dozens of people were gathered around, eagerly watching as it trailed into the field and began to set up camp. Horses were jumping up and down, the elephants were bellowing, people were shouting, wagons were being shifted and the band had given up, defeated by the noise. We stood together at the entrance, our mouths open. Before long, the men began to unfold a gigantic canvas across the grass. Carefully they hammered pegs into the ground and in no time at all, they were pulling and shoving, stretching and positioning the canvas to raise it into the air. Miraculously, the big top appeared before us, like a giant mushroom looming high up above the trees.

A man came over, dressed in a shiny coat. "Ladies and gentlemen, thank you for your patience. The performance will be starting at half-past six this evening. Drag along all your friends and neighbours. It will be a great night's entertainment. Children half price. Something for all the family."

I was just turning to Marie to say something, when suddenly I was caught unceremoniously by the collar and hauled up in the air. "And where do you think you're going?" Mammy planted me back on the ground and peered into my face. "I've been looking everywhere for you. Who said you could come all this way? I only said you could follow them up the street, anything could have happened to you. You've got me light in the head. You're a bold girl, Ann. Home right this minute and no arguing. If you think you're coming back here

25

tonight, you've made a big mistake, there'll be no circus for you now, my lady." Mammy caught Marie and me by the hands and marched us on back up through the town towards home.

I knew I'd done wrong, but was devastated that I might not be able to go. I tried pleading. "Please, Mammy, I'm so sorry, but it was so exciting. Nothing happened to us. See, we're all right. Please Mammy, let me go to the circus."

The went on for some time. There was tears and then more pleading, all through the afternoon and on through tea-time. All my mother would say was, "We'll see."

At five o'clock, Mammy started to get the boys ready to go out to the circus. Pat and Johnjoe stood at the sink to have their faces washed. Mammy was ironing clean clothes for them to wear. There was no word about me. I fretted. Mortified, I climbed on Daddy's knee and whispered to him.

"Please, Daddy, please can I go? I'll really be good. I won't argue with Pat any more and I'll help Mammy as much as I can."

Daddy squeezed me tightly. He looked across at Mammy. "She says she's sorry and won't do it again. She promises to be good."

At his point Pat added rather generously, "Can't Ann go, Mammy?"

We all stared at Mammy, waiting for her decision. I tried once again. "I'll watch the wains and help with the dishes. I'll be good."

My mother looked across at my father, then at the boys and then at me. "All right, Ann, but let this be a lesson to you. Don't disappear for hours on end without asking. Never do that again."

"I promise, Mammy."

I rushed upstairs to get ready, hardly believing that my mother had relented and I would be going to the circus after all.

At six o'clock, we were standing in line to get tickets,

26

along with nearly everyone else in the town. There was chatter and laughter all around; the air was heavy with the sour smell of the animals mixed with sawdust. Children kept running up to the front of the queue trying to get a glimpse inside. At last we had our tickets, then Daddy bought us ice creams and we made our way into the big top. I had never been in a tent before, much less a large one with seats fanning around a central ring. The roof above my head was massive. I felt all wound up and couldn't wait for the fun to begin. Suddenly the ringmaster appeared. He promised that we would be astonished, thrilled and enthralled. There would be all manner of wonderment with trapeze artists, fire eaters, jugglers, clowns, elephants and lions. Pat and I clapped and gasped with delight. Johnjoe stood close to Mammy, unsure of what to expect.

The first act got under way. Four tall grey horses galloped around the ring with riders somersaulting on their backs, the sawdust flying up in clouds as hooves pounded into the ground. Barely a moment later our eyes were turned skyward to watch the flying trapeze.

"Will you look at those women, they haven't got a stitch on," my mother whispered loudly as we gazed at the glamorous trapeze artist who jumped through the air and was caught just in time by a waiting partner. Just then, a dozen clowns appeared, running around the ring, jumping and somersaulting. One came running up to Pat and Johnjoe, who were no longer sitting in their seats but instead kneeling on the ground, peering over the edge of the ring. The clown looked scary. His face was painted white with big coloured lines round his eyes and mouth. He offered the boys balloons. Pat shyly took his, but Johnjoe ran back crying loudly to Mammy, who said, 'Whisht, It's only the clowns."

That night we saw all manner of astonishing things: elephants standing to attention on their hind legs and lions jumping through hoops of fire. I wished it could go on for ever, but too soon, it was over and we headed home through the starlit night full of talk of the evening.

The circus stayed two more days in Falcarragh. I wanted to go again, but Mammy said it would be a waste of money, as we'd seen everything there was to see. That was the only time I ever went to a circus, but that one performance lasted me my whole lifetime.

Chapter 4 - Miraculous Intentions

By the time I was five, we had outgrown our small semi on the main street in Falcarragh and my parents were looking around for something larger and more modern. Mammy had her eye on a new house, one of the pebble-dashed ones being built by the council at the back of the Main Street in Falcarragh. As soon as she was able, she put her name down on the list and was particularly keen to get the end-of-terrace with the side plot, as it would afford her an opportunity to grow her own vegetables and save a bit of money. So, not leaving anything to chance, she urged her friends to say a few decades of the Rosary for her and, not content with just prayers, she lobbied anyone with influence in the town.

Finally though, in one last effort to ensure success, she whispered to me to get my coat, and we set off down the hill towards the cottages. It was a cold, damp day, the clouds moving fast like sailing boats across the sky. Flecks of blue and grey were glistening in the puddles on the ground. My mother held me to her, as, together, we thrust ourselves forward against the wind clattering around our ears.

When we reached the collection of new houses there were still a few workmen around: we could hear carpenters in several of the houses, hammering away. Mammy put her finger to her lips and motioned for me to me to be quiet. Quick as anything she produced a key from her pocket and before I knew it, we were standing in the hallway of the end terrace. Carefully she closed the front door.

"Nobody knows we're here. We have to be very quick and not make a sound. Keep well away from the windows."

I was worried now. What if one of the workmen heard us and came to throw us out. I glanced nervously around. The walls were freshly plastered and there was a pleasant smell of newly sawn wood. The rooms felt fresh and light danced in from the windows, creating patterns on the walls.

As quietly as we could, we wandered from room to room, ducking down beneath the windows in case we'd be spotted by the builders. The house seemed enormous, and as we walked, we could hear our footsteps echoing around the room.

Mammy whispered, "Well, Ann, what do you think of the cottage?"

"It's wonderful. It's even got a bathroom. Will we get it?"

"Please God we will. Isn't half the town praying for us? Only problem is, the other half is on the list."

With that, she produced an envelope from her pocket and handed it to me. I peered inside. It seemed to be full of shiny buttons, but on closer inspection, I could see they were blue Miraculous Medals. Small and dainty, they tinkled inside the envelope when I shook it, the portrait of Our Lady visible on the front, a sign that the wearer would benefit from her grace. I had never seen so many in one place. There must have been forty or fifty. What did Mammy want with all those medals? I had no idea.

Mammy took the envelope back and passed a handful to me. "I've a notion to plant them all around the house. It's sure to work.,' she said.

"What will they do Mammy?"

"They'll do what no earthly power can. They'll perform a miracle."

"A miracle? How, Mammy?"

"Well, Our Lady will look down on the medals and know that we need this house more than anyone else."

"How will she know?"

"Well, I've been saying novenas for the past six months asking for her help. She's surely got the message by now."

I wasn't so sure and anyway I was worried that if we were found planting medals around the house, we'd get into a huge amount of trouble. Mammy seemed unconcerned and instructed me to run upstairs, to slide one under the bath and into any little nooks or crannies I found in the bedrooms.

I was getting more and more nervous, but decided to get it over with as quickly as possible and ran upstairs to do as I was bid. With small fingers, I tentatively pushed a medal in beneath the bath, left one on the corner of a windowsill, and slid several down carefully behind a loose skirting board in each of the bedrooms. Mammy did the same downstairs, so it wasn't long before we found we had used up the whole packet. My mother smiled at me and patted me on the head.

I was ready to go, fearful that any minute now a workman might appear at the door. My Mammy had other ideas though.

"Well done, Ann, you were very good. Kneel down and we'll say a decade of the Rosary. God knows, it never hurts to say one more prayer."

"But Mammy, the men will come. They'll be mad with us," I pleaded.

My mother ignored me and pulled her beads from her pocket.

"The five Joyful Mysteries," she ordered: "Our Father who art in Heaven."

Thankfully, after the Rosary, we made it safely out of the house without anyone knowing. I was so relieved. What a strange picture we must have made on our knees in an empty house, hands clasped together, mouthing the prayer that my mother held so dear.

Later that week we heard the news that we got the end terrace, the one that she wanted so much. Lots of people in the town had an eye on it, but happily in the end it went to us. My mother never had any doubt that it was due to Our Lady's intervention, and specifically to the Miraculous Medals.

In those first weeks after we moved to the cottages, Pat and I could hardly believe our luck. The rooms were large and filled with light, and with our familiar furniture tucked into corners around the house, it felt like home straight away. Everything was sparkling and clean, the rooms smelled fresh, and best of all, the new lino on the floors made a great ice rink as I slid across it in delight. I loved the huge black range which dominated our kitchen and kept us warm and cosy. But most of all, I adored the tall plant stand in the hall, where Mammy had placed a shamrock plant, which cascaded down almost to the floor. When no-one was looking, I used to nibble at the leaves, which tasted sour, like lemons. Best of all, I had a bedroom to myself.

We had three gardens, a lawn at the front, one at the back with a shed, and a massive plot at the side of the house. There was heaps of room to play. Straight away Mammy set to work clearing weeds, digging and planting vegetables in our side plot, and flowers, seeds and bulbs in the front. That summer we enjoyed fresh green cabbages, sweet tender carrots, and floury potatoes with lashings of butter from our own vegetable plot. The flower garden was bursting with bright orange, blood-red and pink dahlias, snow-white gladioli and purple phlox. Around the kitchen window Mammy trained a climbing white rose, its perfume wafting gently indoors. As time went by, I loved to lie in the grass, gazing up at the sun and luxuriating in the sweet aroma of the flowers. Often I fell asleep on the lawn only to wake blissfully in my mammy's arms as I was carried inside.

I adored my new home, and felt happier than ever, but was surprised when one day it was announced that my daddy was leaving us to take up a job in Coventry in England. Although he had never worked away from home before, in our town this was not unusual. Many of my friends' fathers worked in Scotland, only coming home for Christmas and other holidays.

When I came to write this memoir I had little idea about what prompted my father to take the serious step of leaving home to work in England in the late fifties. I'd always assumed it was because they needed the money, but never knew the exact circumstances. At a recent family funeral, I met a cousin of my father's, well into her nineties, who was able to tell me the whole story. Tragically, Dad's partner in the cinema, John Sweeney, died very suddenly of cancer. He was the businessman of the joint project, my dad being more on the practical side. Without John's financial expertise, the profits spiralled downwards. To make matters worse, Dad's other main source of income, tailoring, was also in decline. Cheap, factory-made suits were flooding the market and it seemed there was little demand for the handmade bespoke suits he specialised in. Something had to be done. Hearing of their troubles, my mother's sister, in Coventry, offered a lifeline. She wrote to suggest that Dad come over to the city where opportunities were opening up, with plenty of jobs available. As a result, he applied for a job there as a postman and was very pleased when he got it. It meant he had to go to England on his own, but at least there would be some money coming in at last.

With my father away, most evenings fell into a familiar routine. Mammy and I put my brothers to bed around seven and then we sat down by the fire together to pass the night away. Night after night my mother would click-click-clack in the corner with her knitting and I would play with my dolls. It was a cosy, secure time, with the glow of the firelight in the hearth and the soft murmuring of the radio in the background. I had my mother to myself. I felt blessed.

Sometimes over a cup of cocoa, Mammy would read me Daddy's letters. They were filled with news of his work as a postman, and some of the Donegal people he'd met. Other times she would tell me stories of her girlhood on a farm in Loughfad. The hardship of rising early in the morning to milk the cows before school, working long backbreaking hours in the fields at harvest time. She was the second youngest of seven, and had two brothers and four sisters., and they had all been expected to do their bit on the farm.

One of my favourite tales was of her brother Tommy and his close brush with death, during a bout of rheumatic fever. "Poor Tommy, he was very ill," Mammy told me. "He would have been ten or eleven. Mammy and Daddy were so worried. The doctor was called and he said he could do no more. We were all sitting around Tommy's bed when a knock came to the door. It was Hughdie, a close neighbour. We gave him a cup of tea and he sat at the end of Tommy's bed, chatting away with him and fiddling, from time to time, with the stick he carried. After a while he left and suddenly, to everyone's surprise, Tommy insisted on getting up right away."

When I asked her why this was, she burst out laughing and told me that Hughdie McCloone was the local coffin maker. Apparently, when the family quizzed Tommy about his miraculous recovery, he said ,

"Didn't I see him raising his stick and him measuring me up for my box?"

Possessed of a soft, lilting voice, Mammy loved to sing old Irish ballads whilst scrubbing the floor or washing the dishes, so the house constantly rang to the refrain of "The Wild Colonial Boy" or "The Homes of Donegal." She rarely lost her temper, instead, she had a quiet steeliness about her which we were all in awe of. We seldom answered her back. When I had children of my own she told me that she was most happy when she was pregnant, for she loved babies. She always said she adored the sweet smell of them, their warmth and unquestioning trust. I have a strong recollection of her with Jenny, my youngest, Mammy's head buried in her downy softness, tickling her till she chuckled and gurgled with delight.

Much later, when I was in my teens, my mum told me a little of her life before we all came to Coventry. It was a special time for me when I felt I got to know something of the young woman she'd been, before we had all come along.

After the War, when she was in her early twenties, she worked for a time in England, landing a job as a waitress with Auntie Mary in the Milton Arms Hotel in Cambridge. She loved the work and the independence it gave her. The two sisters attended parties and dances galore as all around them young people threw off the constraints of wartime. Mum was out most weekends till dawn, having a whale of a time.

She was there for about a year when she fell ill. It started with dizzy spells and then shortness of breath. The long hours spent on her feet waiting on tables didn't help. She went to the doctor, but he could find nothing wrong with her. Gradually she became worse, until she was spending more time in bed than at work. Reluctantly, she decided to throw up her job and go to live with my Auntie Mary, who was now married and living in Morley, Yorkshire. Here, her health improved a little and she was able to babysit her nephew, whilst Mary and her husband ran their grocery shop. Her new doctor wasn't happy, although her health was improving, and sent her for a battery of tests at Leeds Royal Infirmary. But Mum didn't really believe there was anything wrong with her and decided to return to Ireland. It was 1951.

Within a few months, she met and married my father and soon found she was pregnant with me. With the onset of the pregnancy, her health failed once again. This time it appeared more serious. She was coughing up blood. Shortly after, she was diagnosed with TB. In those days, thousands of people were dying from the disease and my mother feared for her life. She was admitted to a sanatorium in Killybegs and told to rest. Once there, the physicians were puzzled, because her symptoms seemed inconsistent with the progression of the disease. By contacting her GP in England they learned that the tests in Leeds revealed that she had a leaking heart valve. Alarmingly my parents were informed that she was unlikely to survive the pregnancy. A second opinion from another doctor held out some hope. He said that with complete rest she might have some chance, but then after the baby was born, she would need to have a risky operation on her heart with only a slim chance of survival.

When she was nearing her time my father drove her the two hundred miles to hospital in Dublin for the specialist support she required to deliver the child. On the way she went into labour. The journey, along narrow bumpy roads, was perilous. I can only imagine the fear and terror she must felt as they made their way to the hospital, not knowing if she or her baby would live. I was born shortly after she arrived. A few months later she underwent ground-breaking heart surgery and was told – mistakenly, as it would later transpire – that she was cured and could go on to have as many children as she wanted.

By the time my father left for England, my mother had five children under seven, and she was struggling to cope. She still suffered from dizzy spells and frequently had to take to her bed to rest. To the outside world, Mum was cheerful and outgoing but to her family she was often overwhelmed with feelings of panic and anxiety.

I remember this time vividly. I was only a child, but I was the eldest and anxious to help. I couldn't do very much, only listen and help out with my younger siblings as much as I could.

A great support around this time was Giley, an old lady who lived on the main street in the town. Giley had long silver plaits which hung down her back and dressed in a black dress, with a shawl pulled tightly across her shoulders. When we visited, we were welcomed into her tiny cottage, hazy from the smoke of the turf fire and the steam of the black cauldron, which hung on a hook over it. My mother was always offered the best seat by the fire and Pat, Johnjoe and I would gather round the kitchen table, where we would be presented with a steaming plate of whelks. Mainly oblivious to what was being said, and content with our feast of seafood, we only noticed that their voices rose and fell like a singing kettle on the hob. But I knew all was not well, for sometimes, as they chatted, I would look across at Mammy to see her eyes filled with tears and Giley comforting her.

"God love you, Nora. James will be home soon. You'll find the money from somewhere. You'll see. Now let's have another cup of tea."

In Falcarragh, I never remember feeling poor, but I must have had some notion of it. On one occasion, whilst my dad was away in England, I went into hospital in Letterkenny to have my tonsils out. A neighbour was taking me along with his own two children. As I was preparing to leave, Mum pressed a ten-shilling note into my fist. "Take the money and spend it on something nice for yourself."

I had never had so much money in my life, but knew we could ill afford it. The operation went smoothly, and after a week I was sent home. On the way back, we called into a shop and our neighbour bought a cute little doll for his daughter for five shillings. I was sorely tempted. The ten shillings was burning a hole in my pocket, but I held on to it. When I got home, I handed the note straight back to Mammy. She smiled and gave me a great hug. Her gratitude meant more to me than any doll I could have owned.

A week after my operation, a car pulled up outside. I ran down the path and jumped into my father's arms. Mammy was standing on the doorstep cradling Michael, with Pat, Johnjoe and Charlie clustered around her, holding tightly to the hem of her dress.

"Welcome home, James," she said, smiling broadly, before adding rather alarmingly, "God almighty, you've wasted away to nothing."

Daddy shrugged. "I'm all right. It's grand to see you all again." He turned to us. "You've all grown so big I hardly recognise you. Here, come and say hello to your daddy."

Daddy had been away for six months; he looked different, I hardly recognised him and my brothers suddenly seemed shy in his company, still sheltering behind Mammy's skirts. Eventually, egged on by Mammy, Pat and Johnjoe ran up to him and he bent down and hugged them. We all dragged him inside.

Mammy spoke to us. "Right, I said you could all stay up late to see your daddy, but it's bed time now. Ann, get the caddies ready for their beds whilst I give your daddy his tea."

Daddy drew up a seat by the fire. Mammy was giving out to him. "In the name of God, James, what have you been doing with yourself? You're just skin and bones. Have you been eating?"

My mother was right, even I could see that Daddy's long face seemed longer than ever, his eyes sunk back in his head.

"Of course I have," he protested.

"There's not a pick on you."

"I'm right enough."

"You're like a ghost," Mammy insisted.

Daddy changed the subject. "What's all this about going to live with your mammy in Loughfad?"

"Whisht, I haven't told the wains."

My mother turned away from my father, looking across at me. She could see I was all ears.

"Ann, Give your daddy a big kiss and you and the boys head off to bed. I'll be up a minute. Be sure and say your prayers."

Reluctantly I led my brothers up the stairs, annoyed that I wouldn't hear the rest of the conversation.

Next morning, Mammy was in the kitchen, singing. I rushed downstairs to find that Daddy was still in bed.

"Your Daddy's having a lie in," Mammy explained. "he needs his rest. That job in England takes it out of him."

"When are we going to live with Granny?" I asked.

Where did you hear that, Ann?"

"Daddy said it last night."

"We're not going now. It was just an idea. Granny invited us. But something even better is happening. We're going to go to England. We're going to go to England to be with your daddy. Won't that be grand?" Her face was beaming.

"Where will we live?" I asked.

"We'll have a new house in England. Daddy will have a job. England's great. I was there after the War with Auntie Mary. I loved it. There's shops, parks, buses, trains, everything you could ever want in a month of Sundays. We're sure to be better off."

Mammy made England sound so interesting, like a great adventure, and her words filled me with excitement. None of my friends had been to England and I couldn't wait to tell them I was going. But then I remembered that if I went to England, I wouldn't be able to tell my friends about what it was like, as I would be leaving them behind. For a moment I felt unsure, a bit afraid, but then Mammy reminded me I would make lots of new friends in my new home. As she said it, her eyes lit up. I felt a great wave of joy sweep over me and I knew then I would love England too.

Chapter 5 - An Auction

No sooner had it been announced that we were going to England than we began packing our things into big wooden crates filled with straw. I was determined not to leave anything behind.

"I want to take my Crolly doll and my tea set and my spinning top," I announced.

My doll had been made at the famous toy factory up the road in Crolly. It had been expensive and was my prized possession. She could bend her arms and legs, her head nodded, her eyes opened and closed and she had real hair. My mammy had knitted her a red jumper and a pink skirt with a hat to match, the same as me. I took her everywhere in her pram.

Mammy was firm. "Ann you're putting me stray in the head, just one toy each. We'll get new things in Coventry."

"But you're taking all your things,' I protested. "The knives and forks, the best tea set, the white tablecloths, even the sheets and the pillowcases."

"We're going to need linen," Mammy explained.

"But I'm going to need my toys. What about my dolly's pram? She'll need it."

Mammy was getting impatient with me now and grabbed me by the shoulders. . "There's no two ways about it. We don't have space for everything. We have only a certain number of boxes and when they're full, we have to leave the rest behind. No arguments. You can only take one toy, so you'd better decide what you want to take."

That was the end of it. In a temper, I threw my doll into the packing case. I sulked, it wasn't fair. Pat was upset, too, when he found he couldn't take his tricycle. Pat loved his bike. But Mammy said it was too big. It would take up too much space. He was distraught. Although this tricycle was Pat's, I had always coveted it. To my mind it was a much better toy than any I owned, except, that is, for my doll. My brother and I often had pitched battles over who would ride the tricycle up and down the hill at the front of our house. When eventually we got tired of fighting, we came to an agreement. He rode it up the hill and I rode it down. Pat was so thrilled to own the toy at all, he didn't seem to notice that I got the better deal.

One morning, Mammy shouted from the bottom of the stairs, "Get up."

I sat up in bed and looked out of the window; the road was empty, with no sign of life, only the cows grazing in the field beyond. We weren't going to Coventry till the next day so I couldn't understand why we were up so early.

"There's plenty to do, we've a busy day ahead of us," Mammy announced as I arrived in the kitchen. There were several people there already: friends and neighbours. Together with Daddy they were shifting tables and chairs and stacking them outside in the front garden.

I was alarmed.

"Why are they moving our furniture into the garden?"

"We're having an auction today, Ann, selling everything we can't take with us. Be a good girl, eat up your breakfast and mind the wains while I help Daddy move the tables and chairs."

I had never heard of an auction before, much less been to one. I wondered what it would be like. After breakfast, I gathered my brothers outside on the low stone wall at the front of the house. The sun was just coming up, the sky was turquoise blue. I could see across the fields to the grey slab of Muckish behind the town. I balanced Michael, the baby, on my knee and Charlie, Johnjoe and Pat were quietly sitting beside me as we watched our belongings slowly cover the lawn.

Johnjoe leapt up as he spied something that was stashed away in a box in the corner of the garden.

"That's my yellow lorry. Santy brought that to me. Santy would be cross if we sold it."

He ran over to the box and snatched the small toy out, hiding it under his jumper, before running back to us on the wall.

"You're not supposed to do that. Mammy said we can only take one toy to Coventry. You'll have to put it back," I scolded.

"No-one will see, it's only wee."

"Put it back or I'll tell Mammy."

"I won't, it's mine and Santy gave it to me." Johnjoe clamped his jaws together. I could see he wasn't about to give in.

"All right," I said, "but don't let anyone see you with it."

"They'll just think I'm fat. No-one will know I've still got it," he said.

By now the lawn was covered with haystacks of chairs, tables, cushions and a thousand other things. The sun was beating down; there wasn't a cloud in the sky and I had to shade my eyes against the brightness.

"Look," Pat shouted as he pointed to small groups of people walking down the road.

"Do you think they're coming to the auction?"

Before I could reply, they had descended on our front garden and had begun to sort through our belongings. They were talking, whispering, moving our things about, sitting on chairs, carefully examining bits of furniture. We watched from the safety of the wall, not daring to move.

"A lot of ol' junk," a fat woman in a pink dress whispered loudly to her husband. I was indignant and was just about to go and tell Mammy, when another lady commented on the fine chest of drawers from my parents' bedroom. I felt relieved. Then a man examining the wardrobes from my room muttered to his wife, "Good and sturdy, worth bidding a few bob." I was sure Mammy and Daddy would be pleased to hear that.

Several children had an eye on Pat's tricycle; they sat on it and rode it round the garden several times. Each time, Pat reclaimed it.

Mammy called out to him, exasperated. "Will you leave that bike alone, Pat, you know it's got to be sold."

"But Mammy, it's only wee, we could take it with us. I could carry it."

"We have no room for it, we can't take everything, You can have another one in Coventry."

"I don't want a new one, I want this one."

Pat stamped his foot, grabbed the bike and dragged it back into the house.

I ran in after him.

"Mammy said the bike's to be sold. There's no room on the boat and it has to go."

I grasped the bike and pulled it back into the front garden. Pat ran after me and a tug-of-war developed.

"Now then, you two, calm down. We have to sell the bike. We can't take it with us, so I won't hear another word about it."

Mammy clasped Pat by the hand and pulled him away. Huge tears were sliding down his face. Tears welled up in mine, too, when I thought about what was happening. My dolly's pushchair and pram, Pat's cowboy outfit, Johnjoe's collection of toy cars, Charlie's teddies: they were all going under the hammer. What would we do without them? Although Mammy had promised we could have new ones in Coventry, I didn't feel ready to part with them. Not yet.

At last the auction got going. There was a buzz of anticipation in the air as the first few items were lifted up and offered for sale. The auctioneer was a pal of Daddy's, so there was laughing and joking amongst the bidders as he tried to coax up the prices for us.

"Great wee wardrobe, here, handy for a child, what are my bids? Start me at a fiver."

Laughter all round. "Okay. Who'll give me ten bob?"

Gradually the items were being sold off and the front garden was being emptied of everything, even the old table which had sat outside our back door, long battered by the wind and rain, made a few shillings. My parents beamed. They seemed very content with progress. Eventually, Pat's precious tricycle was being held aloft.

"Ladies and gentlemen," declared the auctioneer, "I have here a child's tricycle, hardly used, what are my bids?"

"Couple of bob," shouted our next-door neighbour.

"Three shillings," cried another.

"Five bob," our neighbour came back. "Sold."

Liam, the boy from next door, rushed up to claim his prize. Pat never said a word, just jammed his lips together. He didn't want anyone to see how upset he was.

I struggled to find some words of comfort.

"It was getting rusty. You were growing out of it anyway, and Mammy said you can have a new one in Coventry. We can all have new toys in Coventry."

Pat just stared at the floor, determined that no-one should see the tears rolling down his face.

At around dinner time the sale ended and my parents stood with the auctioneer, totting up the profits. Daddy was smiling broadly, shaking hands and slapping our auctioneer on the back. Our neighbours were coming up to them, congratulating them.

Giley caught Mammy by the arm and I heard her say, "Are you all right? I never thought the day would come when you'd be leaving us."

"I was just thinking that," Mammy said. I'll miss my garden; I don't think there's much of one where we're going. But it will be a fresh start for us. The family will be together again. The wains need their father."

"I don't blame you," Giley said. "I know how you've all missed James over the past six months. It's a crying shame the government can't find work for our own men here."

"That'll be the day. Haven't Irish men and women been leaving this country for generations, ten families from the town in the last year."

"Well, when it comes down to it, we all need to make a living somehow or other. As I say, I don't blame you and James heading off. If I was a bit younger myself, I might be off there too,'" Giley said.

"Well, Giley, wouldn't you make the fine Englishwoman!" Mammy joked.

"Me? An Englishwoman? Bowing and curtseying to the Queen. Never! St Patrick would turn in his grave."

Both women laughed at the thought.

"Here give me a kiss," Giley said, "And good luck to you now. Don't forget to come back and see us."

Mum and Giley hugged for a very long time before the older woman headed off up the street.

One of Daddy's pals came up to me and the boys, sitting on the wall, then and bending down to talk to us, said, "Are you all looking forward to your new life in Coventry? Sure you'll come back and see us all. Here, have a little something to buy yourselves sweets."

I gasped as I looked down and found he had pressed a sixpence into my palm.

I looked at my parents, my daddy with a protective arm around my mammy's shoulder. She making a final show of thanking our neighbours as they made their way up the street with our few sticks of furniture.

"Well, thanks be to God that's over; there's no going back now. For better or worse, we're on our way to Coventry," Mammy declared.

When everyone had gone home, Mammy began collecting our cases together to take to my father's cousin, where we were staying the night, before our departure the next morning. The older boys were playing out the back and Michael was asleep in his pram. Daddy and I were on our own and now we walked around the house, our steps echoing on the concrete floors.

"Well, what does Daddy's girl think of all this? Will you miss Falcarragh?" Daddy asked.

"I'll miss school, and my friends. I'll miss our house," I volunteered. I suppose I hadn't given it too much thought.

"Aye. I'll miss the place too. We've had a good life here. Nothing will ever be the same."

He looked down at me and squeezed my shoulder.

I gazed up into his eyes. "Do you think we'll ever be back, Daddy?"

"Sure we'll be back, Ann. Please God. Some day. "

"Will it be great in Coventry, Daddy?"

"Well, at least we'll all be together again."

Now the rooms seemed enormous, so bare and empty. I felt a faint glimmer of uncertainty. What if I didn't like Coventry? But then I heard Mammy's voice echoing in my head. "England will be a fresh start for us all. We'll have a nice house and new toys. It will be wonderful."

I couldn't wait.

Chapter 6 - A New Home in Coventry

It was night time as the taxi drew to a halt outside our new house, which was at the end of a row of terraced red-brick houses. We had been travelling for two days and we were all exhausted. The road looked dark and unwelcoming, barely lit by the tall street lamps. Old newspapers, chip papers, bottles and tins cans clattered on the street, blown this way and that by the wind. The place was deserted but for a few drunken souls staggering down the street. Immediately, I hoped there had been some kind of mistake. The building looked forlorn, unkempt, not at all like the pretty whitewashed home I was used to. There was no front garden and next door was a desolate piece of waste ground, full of decomposing rubbish, old tyres and bikes.

We knocked at the door, and a second later a woman with dark curly hair opened it. I didn't recognise her, she was a complete stranger. "Nora, " she exclaimed. "Thanks be to God. We were getting worried. It's very late. We thought maybe you'd missed the boat."

"No, the train was delayed arriving into Coventry, but we're all here, safe and sound"

"Come in. Youse must be frozen." She turned around and called, "Josie, help James with the cases. You children, don't just stand there gawping. Go through to the back room."

We all trailed in. I felt uncertain. Where were we?

"I'll do a nice hot cup of tea for you all and some homemade bread and jam for the children."

Once inside Mammy gathered us all together. "This is your Auntie Katherine and Uncle Josie, and your cousins. Say hello." Auntie Katherine was the youngest in my mother's family, the only one of her siblings living in Coventry.

We murmured a faint hello. I had heard tell of them

47

before, but had never met them.

Our cousins rose and made room for us on the settee. Michael was fast asleep in Mammy's arms, so Auntie Katherine took him and placed him in an armchair by the fire. Our cousins, two boys and a girl, stood in the corner of the room staring at us. Mammy and Daddy were talking nineteen to the dozen with our auntie and uncle. I had a protective arm around Charlie, who cuddled in tightly to me.

Johnjoe was squirming in his seat, turning this way and that, looking around. "Is this Coventry, Mammy?" he asked.

"Yes. At long last."

"I don't like it. I want to go home."

"God love you, poor child. You are home," Auntie Katherine whispered.

Johnjoe looked up at Mammy. She bent down and put her arms around him. "This is your new home, Johnjoe."

His mouth turned down at the edges and he began to sob.

"Want to go home now, Mammy."

"It's all right Johnjoe, you're going to have your tea, look here, lovely scones and blackcurrant jam. You love blackcurrant jam."

"Eat up, don't be shy," my aunt added chirpily as she passed the plate around. We dived on the bread and jam.

"Don't be greedy," Mammy counselled. "And say thank you to your auntie Katherine."

"Thank you," we chorused.

"There's plenty more where that's come from," my aunt beamed. "Now, Nora and James, sit here at the table, I've a nice ham salad all ready. Tuck in. It's been a long journey."

I looked around. The room was dark and gloomy. Dampness glistened on the wallpaper, which was peeling away around the edges. The lino on the floors was cracked and worn. And although the furniture was dusted and clean and the room tidy, to me everything looked tired and old, the opposite of the new house we had just left. I didn't like it here, I thought. I wanted to return to Falcarragh.

"We'll be staying here with Auntie Katherine and Uncle Josie for a few months, then they'll be leaving to go to a new house and we'll have the place to ourselves. Isn't that grand?" My mammy was smiling broadly as she imparted this news to us all. A huge wave of disappointment flooded through me. I envied my cousins. Why couldn't they stay and we leave to go to a new home? I certainly didn't want to stay here.

Auntie Katherine must have sensed something of our misgivings.

"Well, aren't you all big boys and Ann, you're the spitting image of your mother. And the boys, you're really big for your age. Handsome lads. They'll break girls' hearts someday."

"I don't know how to thank you Katherine, you and Josie," Mammy said. "This big feed and letting us stay. I'm so grateful. What we would have done without you? Tears ran down Mammy's face.

"God love you. Think nothing of it. Wouldn't you have done the same for us?" Katherine said. "Now, eat up."

We sat on, licking our lips, staring across at our parents, too shy to make conversation with our cousins.

Charlie began to get grizzly, I tried to soothe him. He was tired.

"Whisht now," I said, "Mammy's having her dinner."

"Mammy, Mammy," Charlie wailed, his small face crumpled like a cabbage.

"Humpty Dumpty sat on a wall Humpty Dumpty had a great fall," I sang, jiggling Charlie up and down on my knee. He was having none of it and continued to cry out for Mammy.

"Here, Ann, he can come and sit on my lap. We'll be finished in a moment," Mammy said.

Charlie held out his arms, pleased to be reunited with his mammy. While my parents ate, they chatted away merrily to my aunt and uncle. We, on the other hand, sat silently, staring into the fire.

"Now you're finished eating we can show you around," Auntie Katherine declared.

Mammy got up and tucked Charlie onto her hip.

"Come on, Ann, you can see the house as well," Auntie Katherine urged. I obeyed, leaving the boys glued to the settee, too scared to move.

There were two large rooms downstairs, the living room and front room. At the back was a kitchen with a deep white sink and a scullery. We climbed the steep stairs off the living room to two large bedrooms. I looked in and a wall of cold air hit me. There was a musty smell in each room and again great damp patches stained the walls. Each bedroom held two double beds dressed with heavy dark blankets and a large wooden wardrobe stood in the corner.

"We thought you could have the one room and we'll have the other," Auntie Katherine said.

"That will be grand. I don't know how to thank you. I'm so grateful." Mammy whispered.

Downstairs again, I glanced at my cousins. They were smiling at me, but I didn't want to know. I was shy and felt strange in their company. An image of our home in Falcarragh popped into my head. Our bright kitchen with the range, the cosy living room decorated with holy pictures, the spacious whitewashed hallway with plants hanging from the windowsills, my pink bedroom. I looked around the dim living room and thought that this was not the new home I had been promised when I left Falcarragh. My mother was sitting at the table, with Charlie on her knee, smiling as though nothing was wrong, but I could see Pat and Johnjoe on the settee, clinging together, holding back the tears.

"Well, time for bed, it's been a long day," Mammy announced. We trailed upstairs. My mother bent down, spreading her arms wide, gathering us together.

"Settle down, get undressed and into bed as quick as you can."

But Johnjoe still wasn't happy. "I want to go home now." He wouldn't stop crying, just kept repeating that he wanted to go home.

Eventually Mammy had heard enough. She grabbed him by the arms and stared angrily into his face. "Stop now, Johnjoe. Stop crying. We can go home. The taxi will be coming back to take us home. But you have to go to bed first. The taxi will come soon. You'll see."

Pat and I looked at each other. We didn't know what to think. I wanted to believe her, but in my heart I knew we were here to stay.

It was freezing cold so we said our prayers quickly and climbed into the double bed. Mammy tucked us in. She turned off the light and went downstairs.

"Do you think we'll be going home tomorrow?" Pat whispered in my ear.

"I don't know. But I don't like it here, I'm cold, these blankets aren't very warm and Johnjoe's cold feet keep rubbing against mine. I don't understand why we had the auction if we're going home."

"Well, Mammy said we were, I bet we are. I'm starving."

"You're always hungry" I accused him. As I closed my eyes I wished with all my heart that we would be moving somewhere else.

Looking back, it must have been a great strain on my aunt and her family to have seven extra bodies in the house, but no-one ever referred to that, or made me feel unwelcome. However, quite recently I asked Johnjoe about his recollection of our first night in Cambridge Street. He was only little, so I was surprised when, like me, he remembered being bitterly disappointed by the house and desperate to go home. Most poignantly, after we all dropped off to sleep, he rose from his bed and stood for a long time, shivering, by the window, looking up and down the road, waiting for the taxi to take him home. It never came.

Chapter 7 - A New World

I awoke to the roar of traffic and the house shuddering around me. It was my first day in Coventry and I'd never heard so much noise in my life. Rushing to the bedroom window I saw two huge cream and red double-decker buses disappearing up the road and around the corner. They seemed to nearly topple over as they raced around the bend.

I dressed and then helped Johnjoe and Charlie get into their clothes. Mammy and Daddy, Pat and the baby, Michael, were up already, so we made our way downstairs. The living room was crowded with people. Michael was bawling his head off and Mammy was trying to soothe him.

"Sit down here at the table. I've a nice feed of porridge for you all," Auntie Katherine instructed.

My cousins got up reluctantly to make way for us. As we were having our breakfast, my aunt explained there was a bus depot at the top of Kepple Street, the road which joined ours, so the house often shook with force of the constant convoy.

We never had double-decker buses in Falcarragh, so I was anxious to see more of them.

"Can I go out to play?" I pleaded as I finished my breakfast.

"No," Mammy replied. "we need to unpack and I want you and Pat to keep Charlie and Johnjoe entertained. You can go out in the afternoon, after dinner, when we're a bit more settled."

"I'm fed up of looking after the boys, I want to go out and play," Pat objected.

"You'll do as you're told and no moaning about it," Mammy said.

"No, I won't,' Pat said. "It's not fair, we're always looking after them."

"I don't need looking after. I'm four, I can look after myself," Johnjoe announced, stamping his foot to emphasise his point.

"See? Johnjoe can look after himself. He doesn't need us."

"You'll get a clip round the ear if you don't give up, now. Right this minute," Mammy said crossly.

"It's not fair," Pat wailed.

"I say what's fair in this house. Here, take Charlie off my knee and go and play with him in the front room. Ann, you can change Michael's nappy for me. He's had his breakfast now, so after he's changed, put him down for a nap."

As a sulking Pat led Charlie and Johnjoe into the front room, Charlie wailed, "Want Ann. Ann play with me."

At two, Charlie was an adorable toddler. To me he seemed like an angel, with his halo of beautiful blond curls. I smiled indulgently at him.

"You go into the room with Pat and I'll come and play hide and seek with you in a few minutes."

Mammy and Auntie Katherine spent all morning unpacking cases, filling the wardrobes and tidying up. Daddy and Uncle Josie were at work and our cousins had disappeared to their friends' houses. Eventually, after lunch, it was time for the younger boys' afternoon nap so after we had done the dishes and helped tidy up, Pat and I headed out of the back door into what we thought was the garden.

Pat stopped short as he encountered a five foot brick wall within touching distance of the back door. It ran the full length of the yard, which was about thirty feet, to a gate at the end. A path led to the gate and we walked down it and peered over the gate, which revealed a narrow alleyway separating the two rows of houses. Our curiosity satisfied, we turned our attention now to the two outhouses which were leaning against the main structure of the house.

Pat flung open the first door.

"What's in here?"

It was a toilet, dark and smelly.

I looked in the next one.

"Uggh, it's full of coal."

Disgusted, I slammed the door shut again and turned my attention to our garden, with its compacted bare earth and a brick path and scattered with old bits of newspaper and rubbish. A couple of old bikes lay in a corner. Planks of wood, tin cans and beer bottles were scattered everywhere. An overflowing dustbin, which stood at the end of the yard, was surrounded by flies and wasps and smelled of rotting vegetables. All around us was neglect and decay. A huge wave of disappointment engulfed me and hot tears sprung to my eyes as I remembered my beloved garden at home. This isn't how Mammy said it would be, I thought. It was meant to be idyllic, better than Falcarragh. Surely we wouldn't be expected to live here, in this dilapidated place. Outside the yard, we could hear the noises of children playing on the street. Pat piled up some of the bits of wood against the wall and we both clambered up onto them, then peered over. There was a gang of children playing football on the road outside. A man passing by on a bicycle shouted at them to get out of his way. They scattered for a minute and then returned to their game. We watched and listened to the screeches of delight from the boys and girls as they tried to score goals, our heads barely peeking out from over the top of the wall.

After about ten minutes, a girl, who had also been watching them, wandered over. She smiled up at us peering down at her. She was wearing a red frilly dress with a white cardigan and a matching bow in her hair. She looked neat and tidy, like she was dressed up to go somewhere. You could see the creases on her clothes where her mother had pressed them.

"Youse want to play?" she offered, in a funny accent, which I had trouble understanding.

She wasn't skinny, like me, but well proportioned. She had long brown hair, brown eyes and the creamiest skin I had ever seen. I liked the look of her.

"I'll ask my mammy."

Five minutes later Pat and I were outside. My brother watched the children playing as I chatted to my new friend.

"What's your name? she demanded.

"My name's Ann. I'm Irish. Mammy and Daddy have come here to live."

"My name's Olwen. My mam's Irish, but my da's from Scotland. I have a brother and two sisters. My brother's deaf. How old are you?"

"I'm seven. I have four brothers. I'm the oldest." Pointing to Pat I said, "he's second oldest and the rest are wee. "

"I'm seven too, but I have an older sister," Olwen replied.

"Olwen is a nice name," I ventured.

"Yes, it's Welsh, but sometimes kids say it's a boys' name."

"I wish I was called something unusual, like Olwen. Everyone's called Ann, I said wistfully."

"Ann's nice too." She smiled broadly at me.

By now the children had finished their game and came over to us. A very tall skinny boy with scraped knees approached Pat.

"Youse wanna play rounders? It's dead easy. You just hit the ball in the air with the bat and run to each base before someone calls you out. If you get round in one, you score a rounder."

It all looked quite complicated to me. I, for one, wasn't eager to play, but Pat seemed keen.

"I'll just watch for now," I said, but Olwen caught my hands and dragged me towards the game.

"Come on, it's simple."

I pulled away.

"Nah, I'll just watch."

I sat down at the edge of the pavement next to where they had marked out their game. The ball was thrown, the batsman launched it up the street and then ran for all he was worth across the road, to first and then second base. Everything stopped as a bus flashed by. A second ball was thrown, Olwen whacked it high in the air. The first batsman completed the round, closely followed by Olwen, who scored a rounder. A cheer went up. Play stopped temporarily again as another bus flew by. When it came to Pats' turn, he managed to hit the ball hard and get to third base. He smiled across at me and I could tell he was enjoying himself. The game was fast and furious, over and back across the road, the boys and girls fearless as they dodged the traffic. I hoped Mammy wasn't watching.

Suddenly the game broke up when several of the players were called in." That was mighty. They said I can play with them tomorrow after school. I'm going to tell Mammy," Pat said.

"Don't tell her you've been running across the road though. She'll be cross," I said.

Olwen came and sat down beside me.

"Let's go round the block, it won't take long. I can show you the area. "

I was about to agree when just then, a taller girl, who looked just like Olwen appeared before us.

"Mam said you're to come in for your tea."

Olwen ignored her and said "I won't be long; I'm just taking Ann on a walk."

"Mam said to come in now. It's getting dark. You'll be in trouble."

"No, I won't. We won't be long, will we, Ann?"

I didn't know what to say. Suddenly Olwen took off down the street shouting at me to follow. I sprinted after her.

"I'm telling on you," Olwen's sister shouted, before disappearing back into the house.

"Won't you get into trouble?" I asked.

"Mam won't mind. It's just her, she's always telling tales. Ignore her. Anyway, it'll only take a few minutes."

Olwen linked her arm in mine as we continued on. I felt

blessed, smitten by this intimacy. Although I'd had a best friend before it had been a boy and I had never enjoyed the same degree of closeness.

For the first time, I began to really take in my surroundings. On either side of us there were rows of dark-red-brick houses with grey slate roofs. Everything towered over us. We could barely see the sky through the evening gloom and the billowing smoke from the chimneys. Dirty, cracked pavements ran alongside the houses, which stretched on down to the end of the street and over another road, where identical rows faded into the distance. There were no front gardens. The buildings looked dismal and neglected. Paint was peeling on all of the windows and doors. The wind pushed a trail of old newspapers, which collected in untidy piles beside the kerb stones. It was like nothing I'd ever seen before. Desolate and unwelcoming, so different from the neat gardens and surrounding fields of the cottages in Falcarragh.

We passed a long brick building where the windows were all blacked out. It looked sinister. I shuddered.

"That's a factory," Olwen explained.

"We don't have them in Ireland. What are they for?"

"I'm not sure. But they queue up in the morning to go to work there. Men round here all work in factories. Mam says we'd all be rich, if they didn't pour it down the drain in the pub at the weekend."

Olwen pointed to a grocery shop further down the street. We crossed the road and went inside. She spent a penny on a bag of sweets and offered me one.

"You can get five Fruit Salads, five Blackjacks, or a couple of gobstoppers for a penny."

Olwen kept up a running commentary, pointing things out as we progressed round the block. I was content to listen. Occasionally we passed a dark 'entry', a pathway between the houses and back yards, filled with more discarded newspapers and broken bottles. The entries looked menacing, unsafe.

"We play Kiss Kat with the boys down the entries. Mam

would go mad if she knew. You won't tell her, will you?" Olwen said.

I could never imagine going down there. A shiver ran through me.

"I've never been to Ireland. What's it like?"

"Not like here. It's hilly. We lived by the sea. It was very quiet. There was no traffic and not so many houses," I explained.

As we turned the corner, we were now back at the top of the road that ran parallel to ours. Olwen pointed to another derelict site, where the earth was uneven and piles of rubbish lay scattered around. Bits of glass and grey slate littered the ground. Now and again, a solitary blade of grass stuck out from behind crumbling bricks.

"That's a bomb site left over from the War. The Germans dropped bombs on the houses and they caught fire. Boys and girls died too. Hundreds of people were killed in the city. It's all right now. The war's over."

"We didn't have a War in Ireland. Were you frightened?" I asked.

"No, I was born after the War."

The thought of war horrified me. It had never entered my head before and was a frightening prospect.

During the War, the German Luftwaffe had bombed the city in a massive air raid that lasted more than ten hours. Wave upon wave of more than 500 aircraft scattered lethal bombs all over Coventry. Five hundred people were killed; hospitals, churches, hotels, cinemas, police stations and ordinary houses were all targeted. The German official news agency described the attack on Coventry as "the most severe in the whole history of the War." Later on, it was rumoured that Churchill had known that the bombers were coming, but didn't want to alert the Germans to the fact that the British had broken the codes on the secret Enigma machine. So the city was sacrificed. Buildings lay in ruin, street upon street had been demolished. Hillfields, where we lived later, was one of the worst hit: there, a least one building on every street had been reduced to rubble.

In those early years in Coventry, the presence of these neglected bomb sites on every street in our neighbourhood was a constant reminder to me of the reality of war. I fretted constantly that the bombers might return and I would wake up at night, convinced that planes were overhead and that we'd be killed in our beds. My mother also hated the bomb sites. For her, they were a symbol of the decay and neglect that characterised the area, that made it notorious throughout the city. Sadly, it wasn't until after Mum died that the bomb sites were eventually cleaned up. Gravel paths were laid upon them, with shrubs and grass. My mother would have approved of that, especially as there was one next door to our house.

"Which school will you be going to?" Olwen asked.

"I don't know." I hadn't thought of school.

"I go to St Mary's. Maybe you'll go there too. We could walk to school together. We could be best friends."

The thought of having a best friend so soon after my arrival thrilled me. I smiled and hoped that I, too, would be going to St Mary's.

As we walked down the road to the back of our houses I could see a head bobbing up and down at the gate next door to ours. It was a small, thin, dark-haired woman. She looked cross, her lips clamped together tightly, her cheeks sucked in. When she saw us, she said,

"You're a bold girl, Olwen. Why didn't you come in when Jessie called you? I've been looking for you. It's getting dark now. Who knows what might have happened to you in this neighbourhood? Get in this gate at once. And don't let me hear a peep out of you. And you," she said, turning her fury on me, "Get home to your mother; you shouldn't be out at this time of night."

I ran in through the gate as fast as I could, mortified at

her words.

Mammy was waiting at the back door.

"Where in God's name have you been? Patrick was in ages ago!"

As I lay in the bed that night, I wished that when I woke up, I would find myself back in my cosy bed in Falcarragh, in our bright modern house with its views over Muckish Mountain . But then, I thought, I wouldn't make friends with Olwen if I went home. It would be great to have a pal of my age to play with and to walk to school with. My best friend in Falcarragh was Donald. Our mothers were great friends and were constantly in and out of each other's houses. Donald and I had known each other since we were in nappies. But when I came out of school on just my third day there, there was a crowd of children standing around the gate. A teacher was guarding something that lay beneath a coat on the ground.

"Get home now as quick as you can and be careful on the road. Wee Donald's been killed, he's run out and been knocked over by a car."

There was no sign of blood. I couldn't understand how it could have happened so quickly, how he could be running out of school one minute and gone the next. I had no concept of dying. At first, I hardly believed it was him, under the coat. It seemed so unreal, like a dream. A few days later we went to his house to pay our respects and found him laid on a table in a small coffin. He wore a white satin gown, his little hands clasped round a Rosary. He looked so perfect, not a scratch on him. His eyes were closed and his hair was combed to one side. I still couldn't believe he was dead. I expected that any minute he would open his eyes and jump up. I had never known anyone before who'd died. Mammy said he was an angel in heaven. I pictured him with wings, floating on a cloud.

Since he had died I hadn't had a proper best friend, playing instead with different girls and boys. I missed him.

Now, Olwen had promised me that we could be best friends. She said she would teach me to play "two ball" up against the wall and that we could play hopscotch together. It all sounded like fun. Perhaps England wasn't going to be so bad after all.

Chapter 8 - Settling In

When we arrived in Coventry, the area where we settled, Hillfields, had one of the worst reputations in the city. Crime was rife and people didn't walk the streets alone after dark. Later at secondary school when anyone asked me which area of the city I was from I would be vague and say, "Just off the Stoney Stanton Road." I was too ashamed to admit I was from Hillfields.

One of the poorest districts in Coventry, most of the houses there were slum dwellings and most of its inhabitants migrant workers from Ireland, the north of England and Scotland. However, in spite of its reputation, the Hillfields area had always been a huge attraction for labour from around the British Isles, mainly because of the development of different and diverse industries there down the ages. Two hundred years earlier families had arrived to weave silk and were housed in appalling conditions directly underneath their place of work. These were four-storey dwellings with workshops on the top floor, which led to them having the name "top shops."

The start of the 20th century saw the beginning of the motor industry and soon Hillfields became home to a host of automotive manufacturers. Once again families flocked in, renting cheap, overcrowded accommodation. Less than a decade before we arrived, the housing was so poor in Hillfields that the council declared that half of the houses there were unfit for human habitation. Impoverished as our house was, it was not as bad as many at the time, which had no running water and very poor sanitation.

It wasn't all dire though. There was Primrose Hill Street, a mile from where we lived, where we did our shopping. The street was lined with haberdashers, hardware stores, butcher's, grocer's and greengrocer's shops. There were trestle tables covered with fruit and vegetables along the pavements. Every Saturday morning these pavements were jammed with women and children, dashing from one shop to the next, their bags weighed down with groceries. As a youngster fresh from the countryside, I had never seen such an abundance or variety of wares all in the same place. It was mesmerising. Carrots, cauliflowers, potatoes, apples, oranges, tomatoes, all beautifully displayed, the fruit polished and glinting in tall pyramids, with signs denoting the prices.

These days everything is self-service. Back then, you wouldn't dare pick up an apple or an orange to inspect it, but had to wait patiently for the assistant to select it for you. By the end of the sixties this was changing. The newest immigrants, Asian women, came to the shops poking and prodding the vegetables, checking if they were fresh before taking them to the till to be weighed. My mother was scandalised.

Further up, where the street changed its name to Victoria Road, was the Home and Colonial Stores. It declared its status with its name picked out in grand gold lettering on black marble. This was the place we did most of our grocery and meat shopping. The window was stacked high with rows of neatly arranged, brightly coloured jams, boxes and tins of food. Posters promoting the bargains of the day decorated the glass. Inside, shoppers worshipped at the altars of polished wooden counters, with beautifully inscribed advertising mirrors at the back. Sawdust was sprinkled liberally over the floor. All the assistants were enveloped in long white aprons and wore hairnets to complete the image of cleanliness, their rosy cheeks an advertisement for the quality of food on offer. Here, we bought streaky bacon, neck of lamb, ribs of pork, anything cheap, which Mammy turned into stews and soups. Often I was sent to get the "messages" on my own, particularly when my mum was ill. I loved having this great responsibility, even if I was once embarrassed by the assistant, who remarked that I was too young to be carrying the shopping home on my own.

Most of all I loved to go into the haberdashery store, where I could point and a smiling assistant would remove trays of brightly coloured ribbons and hankies from beneath deep glass counters. Before arriving in Coventry, the world of shops had meant nothing to me, but here in Primrose Hill Street, I discovered they could take you out of your world, transport you somewhere else, somewhere full of wonder and delight.

Someone visiting Primrose Hill Street today would see a very different picture, with the shops of my childhood replaced by new housing, community buildings and the tower blocks built in the seventies. The few shops remaining advertise food for the latest wave of poor immigrant families, but to me they seem to me to lack the colour and vibrancy of the ones they replaced.

My first visit to a restaurant over forty years ago was on Primrose Hill Street. My boyfriend, later my husband, took me to The Captain's Table, where he impressed me by introducing me to fine dining. I was seventeen. We had prawn cocktail to start, followed by coq au vin, and for dessert, Black Forest gateau. I felt like the Queen.

I don't remember the first time I visited Coventry city centre, but I do remember the sense of delight at being just a short bus ride from the shopping precinct in town. It was the first pedestrian shopping area in Europe and I clearly remember it being something of a tourist destination and the pride and joy of the city. Before visiting Belfast, I'd never seen a city and suddenly I was living in one. I was in awe. I loved to catch the bus and wander around by myself. Coventry was famous for its association with Lady Godiva and at the top of the precinct stood a fine statue of the lady naked on her horse, overlooked by a mechanical Peeping Tom, who popped out every few minutes to catch a sneaky glimpse of her. As you went further into the shopping centre, you were enveloped by such luminaries as Woolworths,

Marks and Spencer, British Home Stores and dozens of other shops selling everything you could possibly want.

For hours I would linger over the jewellery counter in Woolworths, trying on rings and necklaces I could never afford. On one occasion, I was hovering by the jewellery, admiring a swanky, brightly coloured bracelet when Mrs Mangan, a neighbour, pounced on me, firing questions at me about my family. I was flabbergasted, as she always seemed rather stuck-up, but she was smiling warmly at me, trying to engage me in conversation. To my dismay, her interrogation went on for some time, till eventually, feeling she would never shut up, I excused myself, saying I had to dash off to buy something for my mother. It was only afterwards that I wondered if she thought I was about to steal the bracelet, and that explained her rather odd behaviour. At first I was insulted by the idea that she considered me a thief, but then touched that she cared enough to try and stop me.

Away from the magic of the shops, those first few months in Hillfields, sharing a house with Auntie Katherine and her family, were tricky. Damp and overcrowded, it was impossible to relax and treat the place like home. With twelve people squeezed into a two-bedroomed terrace, someone was always watching. There was no privacy. In Donegal, we had a new three-bedroomed home, with a bathroom and inside toilet. It was warm and bright. In Coventry, it was the opposite. Clothes trailed over every surface and finding a seat to call your own was a constant battle. In the morning, we shivered and crossed our legs, waiting in the queue to go to the outside toilet. There was no hot water and very little warmth. To top it all, we were plagued by mice and had to set traps all over the house to catch them. One day, there was a big commotion in the house when a mouse ran up my uncle's leg. He roared loudly, shaking it out on the lino, before dispatching it with a poker.

We longed to have the place to ourselves and I for one

was relieved when the mortgage came through on my aunt's new house, which they had bought a little while earlier, and they began packing to leave. To celebrate, my parents went out and bought a few sticks of furniture. Unlike many of the people working in the factories earning good wages, my dad's wage as a postman was poor. My parents had scrabbled together a deposit on our house with money raised from the sale of dad's share of his cinema, but every month they struggled to pay the mortgage. Money was tight and we couldn't afford much, so we bought from second-hand shops. These were dark, dusty places, musty smelling, bursting with old wardrobes, dressing tables, creaky beds, sewing machines and lamps. Inside, there would always be a man in a dirty old sweater sitting at a wonky desk, puffing away on a Woodbine. They were reluctant sales assistants, rising slowly and deliberately from their chairs, in no hurry to help. Once they were up though, they seemed to know every piece of furniture intimately; its history and its value, and they drove a hard bargain.

"Quality piece that, had to pay dear for it. Couldn't take less than a ten bob note."

Now, I helped Mammy to choose a double bed, a table, a wardrobe and some chairs. They were the cheapest we could get, but nice all the same because they were actually ours. At last, we had the place to ourselves, and we went about rearranging the furniture and tidying up. We even set about repairing the few things my aunt had left behind. The settee, with its springs coming through the lining, we piled with extra cushions. We re-covered the dining chairs with some offcuts of fake leather that we bought in the market.

Gradually the house was taking shape and becoming our home; nothing like as good as our old home in Falcarragh, but a home all the same.

I had never been overly conscious of the fact that we were poor in Donegal, but in Coventry I was constantly reminded of it. When our first winter came, we huddled, frozen, beneath frayed grey army blankets, bought second-hand from Riddy's army surplus store, and watched our breath rising in spirals above us. The windows were laced with ice, the dampness seeping through the ceiling. Our parents and Michael the baby were in one room and the three boys and I were in two double beds in the other. In Falcarragh, I had a room and a bed to myself, but now I must share a bed with Pat.

Every morning before breakfast we huddled around the coal fire, trying to get warm. Habitually, Mammy would remove the fireguard so we could get closer to the heat. This routine went on for years, with the family continuing to grow with the birth of two more children, my baby sisters, Carol and Mary. One morning in particular, my mother removed the fireguard and we crowded around, pushing and shoving to get warm. Unexpectedly Carol, who was just a toddler, tumbled into the fire. She didn't have her nappy on so her bare bottom hit the red-hot grate. She let out a huge scream and my mother ran to her, scooping her up from the floor.

"Jesus, Mary and Joseph. What'll we do? The writing on the grate is tattooed on her wee bottom," Mammy cried.

Sure enough, you could see the advertising slogan clearly displayed on Carol's burning flesh.

"Oh God, what'll we do?" Mammy wailed again.

I ran into the kitchen, shouting over my shoulder, "I know, we'll put egg white on it. That's sure to help."

Egg white had long been a cure for burns in our house. I quickly broke some eggs into a bowl, carefully separating the whites. Mammy plastered them all over Carol's scalded bottom. We all stood around, too shocked to say anything, whilst my mother sat cradling Carol, praying she would be all right. Eventually, worn out by her own screaming, my little sister fell into a fitful sleep.

The episode was a terrifying one, especially for my mother, who never left the fireguard off again. I recently asked my sister if the branding was still visible - she assured me it wasn't.

Although I was thrilled by some elements of my new life, I still longed to be back at home in Donegal. At night, I dreamed I was walking along the beach, the sounds of the waves lapping against the shore, the sun beating down. Sometimes I'd imagine I was playing in the garden, dragging my bare feet through the damp grass, bending down to catch the scent of the flowers growing around the window.

Now, it seemed my life was spent looking backwards, remembering what I'd lost. It wasn't the people I missed, but the place. My only compensation was that the people I loved most were still with me. At least, for the time being, I had that. The beauty and magnificence of my surroundings, which I'd taken for granted, were lost to me now. Another time, another world far away.

Chapter 9 - St Mary's

On a sunny autumn morning a few weeks after we arrived from Donegal, Pat and I set out with Mammy for our first day at our new school. We were full of excitement and enthusiasm. I had a brand new dress which I wore with a hand-knitted white cardigan and Pat wore a checked shirt with neatly pressed shorts. We skipped along the road, with no backward glances, eager to get there before the bell rang at 9 a.m.

The beginning of our route was a familiar one, past red-brick terraces the same as ours, but then we diverged and came upon a row of tall, sinister-looking tenements with many of the windows broken or boarded up. The dwellings looked precarious, as if they might tumble at any minute, like tired cardboard boxes. At the back of the tenements, we could see cobbled courtyards with women queuing at standpipes, filling buckets with cold water. The yards were criss-crossed by washing lines and, in underneath them, dirty looking toddlers, nappies hanging down, ran about, crying for their mammies. It was the type of scene I'd witnessed occasionally on the roadside in Donegal, when tinkers had parked up for the night.

Things improved slightly as we got closer to the school. There was a huge grassy area nearby with swings and roundabouts that Mammy said was a park. She promised we could go and play there at the weekend.

When we turned the final corner and approached the school, I could hear shouting and screeching and gripped Mammy's hand tightly as we were encircled by hundreds of boys and girls jostling one another. I had never seen so many children in one place in my life. The building was huge, it towered over us. It was modern, grey, and had two storeys, with dozens of large windows all facing the surrounding playgrounds and streets. My school in Falcarragh could have fitted into this one twenty times over.

I felt nervous, my earlier enthusiasm giving way to a sense of anxiety about what lay ahead. We pushed through the crowds and made our way to the headmaster's office. There were corridors in every direction. It all looked brand new, shiny and bright. The walls were lined with children's paintings and at each corner there were religious statues with offerings of flowers at their feet.

We knocked at the door of the headmaster's office and his secretary came out and asked us to sit outside. All around us was the clamouring of hundreds of children, squealing and shouting, laughing and joking as they lined up in the playgrounds ready to start the day. There was a smell of polish and a whiff of new books in the air. The teachers blew their whistles and there was silence for a few minutes, followed by the sound of marching. I felt light-headed, excited but anxious at the same time. Pat seemed bored and was scuffing his shoes over and back across the floor. Mammy grew impatient with him and told him to stop. He flounced down angrily on his seat.

As I sat waiting, I reflected how different this was to my old school in Falcarragh, where in winter, we huddled together round an open fire, trying to keep warm. There, our teacher was forever swatting mice with a poker and shovelling them into the fire. I couldn't envisage many mice in this swanky new building.

The headmaster finally appeared and invited us into his office. He was a very tall, thin man with very little hair, and was dressed in a brown shiny suit. He looked strict and scary. I clutched my mammy's hand tightly. Pat stood in the corner, reluctant to move to the centre of the room.

Mammy spoke up. "This is Pat and Ann."

The headmaster looked at each of us in turn and then his voice boomed out. "And how old are you two children?"

"I'm seven," I squeaked.

"I'm five and we're Irish," Pat announced, rather

70

proudly.

"Well, I won't hold that against you. You're a big boy, the same size as your sister. Are you sure you're only five?" the headmaster said.

"Mammy says I'm big for my age. I'll soon be taller than Ann, too."

Pat turned round and smirked across at me. It didn't please me one bit. With gangly arms and legs too long for his short body, Pat was threatening to overtake me in height, a fact that I was reluctant to own up to. In reprisal, I stuck my tongue out at him only to get a censoring look from my mammy. Thankfully, the headmaster, who was studying some papers on his desk, didn't notice. Now, Mammy informed him that we'd just arrived in Coventry from Donegal and had been told to come today to register for school. He invited her to sit down, asked for our birth certificates and took some details. He filled out some forms and then looked up.

"Everything seems to be in order. You can start now. Young Pat in the infants class and Ann to Miss Lynch in the juniors."

He then went to the door and summoned his secretary to take us to our respective classes.

Outside his office, all had fallen quiet. Reluctantly we said our goodbyes to Mammy.

"Don't lose your dinner money and I'll see you both later. Be sure and wait for me at the school gates," she said, waving us goodbye.

After dropping Pat at his classroom, the headmaster's secretary and I walked to a temporary prefab building in the schoolyard and knocked on the door, to be greeted by a sea of faces, all staring in my direction. I hung my head, too shy to look them in the eye. In Falcarragh, there were ten in my class, here, there were at least forty. My teacher, who introduced herself as Miss Lynch, made a great fuss of me and asked me to sit down next to a girl called Margaret. She looked friendly and had bright red hair with a sprinkling of freckles dotted around her face.

The register was called out. Most of the names were familiar Irish ones, Kelly, McGee, O'Malley. Then, we started our lessons. First, it was reading, and each child had to read out loud. When it came to my turn, I stumbled over my sentences, barely understanding one word in three. From around the room I could feel the other boys and girls staring at me and smirking. I was so embarrassed. I desperately wanted to get up and leave. Thankfully, for the next lesson, I managed to get most of my sums right and felt my confidence return, only to find it shattered when we did a spelling test and I only got one spelling out of ten right. It was 'piano', I could spell piano.

I jumped as the sound of the dinner bell pierced the silence. I was relieved. We all filed out for lunch. In the dinner hall, we queued for a plate of food each. It was lumpy potatoes with cabbage and cold meat. It smelled vile and made me want to vomit. I wasn't used to school dinners. In Falcarragh, we had taken a packed lunch. Afterwards, in the playground, I looked around for Olwen; I saw that she was with her friends and I didn't feel confident enough to join them, so I sat alone on the steps watching the others playing. After a while a group of girls from my class came up. They fired questions at me. Was I staying? Did I like the school? I just smiled and nodded at most of the questions. Worriedly, I scanned the playground for any sign of Pat. A girl with horn-rimmed glasses and long pale hair told me the infants played in a different playground. I hoped he was all right. The girls invited me to join in the skipping, but before I could, the bell rang again. We filed into rows in the playground and marched back to our classroom.

That afternoon, the whole class went country dancing in the hall. Miss Lynch paired me up with a boy called John. He was smartly dressed, tall and good looking. I was delighted to have such a fine partner, but didn't know any of the dances. I kept getting it all wrong, but John was patient and considerate, taking my hand gently in his as we skipped around the room.

At three o'clock Mammy was waiting for both of us at the gate. She was smiling broadly. "Well, Ann. Did the teacher say you were good today?"

I was reluctant to tell her how difficult I had found it, so I said, "It was all right. I didn't like the school dinners. The mashed potatoes were all lumpy." I revealed nothing of my failure in reading or spelling.

However, Pat was bursting with news of his day. "Dinner was great. I ate it all up. The dinner lady gave me seconds. We played with toys and painted pictures. It wasn't hard. I had milk at break time. I made friends with some boys. Look, I've drawn a picture."

"Well, isn't that grand," Mammy cooed, putting her arm round Pat. "It's our house in Falcarragh and Muckish Mountain in the distance. Well done."

Seeing the painting made me feel homesick. I longed to be back there. I wasn't sure I liked this new school: the lessons were hard. I was annoyed. Why couldn't I have played with toys and drawn pictures, instead of reading and spelling? I didn't think it was fair.

Before long we settled into a routine and instead of Mammy taking us, Pat and I set off every morning with a group of children from our street to walk the mile or so to school. Every day, we were given a penny to buy sweets and stopped at a shop not far from the school. It was very dark inside, the daylight barely squinting through the half-drawn blinds. However, stacked on shelves covering the walls, were huge jars of brightly coloured boiled sweets, Barley Sugars, Kola Kubes, and toffees wrapped in shiny paper. My mouth watered at the sight of them, but they were too expensive for us. Instead, we headed to the front counter, where, together with the morning's newspapers, they kept the penny sweets.

"Two gob stoppers, please, Mister" we'd ask, or, "Five

fruits salads and no black ones."

I loved the daily ritual of spending my pocket money on a gobstopper or a lolly. It was something to look forward to, one of the things which made my school days bearable.

Over the months, I developed an ambivalent attitude to St Mary's. On the one hand, I loved the clean, bright building, the airy classrooms and my teacher. But on the other hand, I was hugely disappointed in my performance. In Falcarragh, I did as well as my other classmates, but here I found that, to my horror, I was far behind the rest of them. I could barely read the books we used, or spell any of the words when it came to spelling tests. I loathed and hated school dinners and very rarely ate anything, but most upsetting of all was that Olwen wasn't even in my class. At first I thought we could be together in the playground, but she made it clear she wanted to be with her friends. I didn't blame her, but was devastated. In desperation, I tried to make friends with other girls, but found that after the novelty of being the new girl in the class had worn off, no-one seemed interested in me. Margaret, whom I sat beside, would sometimes take pity on me and invite me to play. But most of the time I wandered around on my own. At home, I had never been short of pals, now I felt lonely and self-conscious. No-one wanted to be my friend.

One day, when I had only been at the school for a few months, a gang of girls came up to me. The tallest, a fat girl with mean, piercing eyes, demanded that I speak to them. I didn't know what they meant, so tried to get away, but they grabbed me and held onto me.

"Just say something. Say anything so we can hear that funny accent."

I was incensed. "I haven't got a funny accent. I can speak perfectly well."

"Yes, you have. You sound like you've just come off the boat. We can hardly understand you," said the mean girl. "You should speak English like the rest of us."

"I am speaking English," I protested.

She wasn't impressed and poked me in the ribs saying, "I'm going to tell everyone not to speak to you until you learn English."

I didn't recognise her; she wasn't in my class. I felt frightened and started to cry. I turned around and Olwen suddenly appeared at my elbow.

"Leave her alone. She's not doing any harm. I'm going to tell the teacher on you."

From nowhere a crowd of girls, classmates of Olwen's, surrounded my tormentors. My friend took the lead: "If you dare speak to her again, we'll come and get you. There are more of us than you. Ann's friends will get you, too. So you'd better be careful."

The bullies ran off. I was invited to play with Olwen and her friends and was jubilant. My best friend had rescued me. I felt so grateful; no-one at school had ever stood up for me like that before.

Later, I thought about what they'd said about my Irish accent and realised for the first time that I was different to my schoolmates. Like my dad had said on the boat, I was Irish. Although the boys and girls in St Mary's had Irish names, it was their parents who were actually Irish. The majority of the children had been born and raised in Coventry. They had grown up in the city and fitted right in. With dismay, I realised I was the odd one out, an Irish girl with a funny accent. I still felt proud of where I'd come from, but at the same time was desperate to fit in. I wanted to make friends, to be good at my lessons, but mainly I wanted to be like all the rest of them.

St Mary's was a Catholic school and there was an inevitable concentration on religion. We were taught our catechism by rote and often a priest came to test us on it. The Fathers stressed that we had to be good and not tell lies or disobey our teachers. Frighteningly they preached that my soul was in mortal danger if I committed a sin, any sin, no matter how small. I was regularly reminded that if I wasn't well behaved, I would end up in purgatory, or worse still, in the burning fires of hell. I was consumed with dread and prayed constantly to the Virgin to keep me free from sin and my soul pure.

Religion was all-pervading in the school and on saints' days we were taken to Masses organised specifically for us at the local church. After assembly, we would line up in the playground, class by class, in twos, and led by the teachers, walk in an orderly fashion the half-mile to church.

My parents had a rather relaxed attitude to education: they always said, "Just do your best." Nonetheless, they were disappointed when I turned in reports filled mainly with Cs and Ds. I've often wondered about why I did so poorly at junior school and surmised that it could have had much to do with my poor reading skills. I'm not dyslexic, but there is certainly a family difficulty with spelling and reading. The rest of my brothers followed Pat and me to St Mary's, but only Johnjoe seemed to excel there and pass his eleven-plus, which would guarantee him entry to a grammar school. Michael was a poor speller, like me, and he would put his hand up to go to the toilet when spelling tests began. He lived in constant fear of the cane and having his knuckles rapped with a ruler when he got his sums wrong. They were fond of corporal punishment at St Mary's and I remember one occasion when I went into Pat's class to say he wasn't coming to school that day, and his teacher caned me for nothing at all.

Not all the memories are unpleasant, though. Charlie recounts rather cheekily asking his teacher if he could have a brightly painted wooden toy train, which sat at the front of his classroom. I suppose he didn't have many toys at home and had coveted the train all year. His teacher seemingly said nothing, but at the end of term presented it to Charlie and he and Pat proudly carried it home.

The slum clearance in the sixties and seventies marked

the beginning of the end for St Mary's, like many of the familiar institutions of my childhood. The Irish immigrant families, whose children had made up the majority attending the school, were dispersed to council estates in Wood End and Bell Green, on the edge of the city. The new wave of immigrants into Hillfields were Asian. There was no longer a need for a large Catholic primary school. A smaller, more modern primary school, St Benedict's, was built in the 1970s, which gradually took over from St Mary's and by 2005, there was a building site where St Mary's once stood, its dereliction a symbol of the disappearance of the Irish Catholic community that had been so much a part of life in Coventry in the middle of the 20th century.

Chapter 10 - Sunday Mass

A central part of the Irish Catholic community's identity was the local church. Today the congregations, even in Catholic churches, have dwindled and the churches are half-empty, often with one priest shared between several parishes. In the late fifties and sixties it was entirely different. The Catholic church in Hillfields, St Mary's, was swollen with Irish immigrants intent on fulfilling their obligations. They came from every direction and a queue formed to get into the church, snaking down the street and around the corner. Back then, there were five Sunday Masses from seven-thirty up to noon. My dad always went to the later one, but Mum, believing earliness was next to Godliness, roused the rest of us and we attended Mass either at seven-thirty or nine o'clock.

The church was located in the heart of the inner city, surrounded by Victorian terraced housing: tall gloomy factories and bomb sites. Waiting outside for the service to begin, we chatted excitedly and joked with our friends, whilst the grown-ups swapped news and stories with neighbours about the living and the dead at home in Ireland.

When we had finally pushed and shoved our way into the church, I gazed with wonder at the green baize-topped table spilling over with threepenny bits and shiny silver sixpences, payment for *The Universe*, the Catholic paper. I longed to hold the coins, to manipulate them around the table, to grab handfuls in my fists. I'd never seen so much money in my life. Mum scrimped and saved every penny she could, but here was more money than we had in our house in a month. Every Sunday! I longed to gather it all up in my pockets and present it to her. She who, like many of the others attending Mass, struggled to feed her family.

In sharp contrast to the grimy streets outside, St Mary's was a haven of beauty and tranquillity. Painted bright lemon inside, it was light and airy when the sun shone through the stained-glass windows. In the porch and little side chapels, kindly statues of Our Lord, the Virgin Mary and St Joseph smiled down on us. And in the church itself, the wide wooden benches stretched up the aisle to the main altar, which was covered with a white cloth and decorated with flickering candles, flowers and polished gold crucifixes. The blooms were artfully arranged by the Mothers' Union, and always sent a soft hint of perfume down the church, which reminded me of my granny's in Loughfad.

Every week we sat in the same seat, squashed tightly into pews a few rows from the front, where we got the best view. As we shuffled around, we glanced this way and that, looking to see who had made it on time and who was standing up at the back, too late to claim a pew. We would be whispering and gossiping till eventually the bell signalling the start of Mass was rung and the priest appeared from the sacristy. As a child, the service passed in a haze of kneeling, standing up and fidgeting. I rarely paid attention, except, that is, when it came to the sermon. Fierce and sometimes terrifying, the priest preached relentlessly on the evils of sin, the dangers of temptation and the ungodly English world around us. He said the devil lurked everywhere: in social clubs, in the English Sunday newspapers, and especially on TV. He was in our thoughts, our words our actions. Nowhere was safe from his pervasive evil.

Today, we witness some Muslim clerics preaching much the same kinds of sermon to the new generation of immigrants into Britain. We are shocked and denounce heartily their barbaric attitudes to the modern world, but the Catholic Church was similar in my young days. Terrified of being tempted, I shivered as I contemplated giving into the lure of the ungodly world around me. I rushed to make my confession every week, convinced I would burn in hell if I didn't. I prayed endlessly to the baby Jesus to watch over me, to keep my immortal soul safe from sin and the temptations that lurked all around.

Another favourite topic on Sundays was the lack of funds at the church and the need for families to give more. Each week the priest urged us to be generous and give as much as we could. But most people living in the area had very little to give. Many were sending funds home to their families, others lived on low wages, in damp overcrowded accommodation, with barely a penny to spare. Our Mum, however, was not about to be shamed if someone noticed she had nothing for the collection plate, so every week the budget was stretched to breaking point as money was found for the donation.

Although we were not the most pious, we always went to Sunday Mass and sometimes even went to Benediction. I particularly enjoyed the Latin singing at Benediction and the smell of the thurible held aloft by the priest as he led us in our evening prayers. Over the years, Pat, Johnjoe, Charlie and then Michael became altar boys. I know that secretly my mother always entertained high hopes of one of them becoming a priest. It was not to be. But, every Sunday I could see the pride on her face as one of them led the priest out of the sacristy in his smart black and white robes.

At home, most nights, we all knelt down and said the Rosary. Mum had been raised on the Rosary: it was an important part of traditional Irish rural life, which she brought with her to Coventry. She always took the lead, singing out the Hail Marys, as heads bowed, we mumbled our replies into our Rosary beads. To Mum, the prayer was a great comfort. It reminded her of Donegal, of her family, of her childhood, when the world was a much simpler place. She prayed lovingly on a set of beads her father had brought home from America. She kept them with her always. Small, yellow crystal beads, worn away over the years. Often, I would arrive home to find her alone, sitting in her chair in the dark, fingering those beads, reciting her prayers, the Sacred Heart lamp glimmering from the wall.

As time went by and my brothers and sisters were growing up, we became only too willing to relinquish the customs and practices that my parents had brought from Ireland. We were becoming Coventry kids. In the evening, when it was time for the Rosary, we protested loudly to my mother that it wasn't cool to spend time on your knees praying. Instead we headed out with our mates to the discos and pubs. Except, that is, on a cold March day in 1982, the night my mother died. By then I was married with children of my own. Mum, aged only 59, had gone into hospital to have a heart operation, but never survived the surgery. My brother Michael telephoned me with the news: "Mum's passed away."

I was numb with shock. I had been with her the night before and she seemed full of optimism. Now, with the news that she had died, I desperately needed to be near the rest of my family. As I entered my old home, I was surprised to find my father and brothers and sisters on their knees, beads pressed tightly to their chest, holding back the tears, my father for once, leading them in the Rosary. It was the saddest thing I ever saw.

Chapter 11- The Chosen Ones

At St Mary's, there was always huge excitement about who would be the May Queen and her attendants. As I had only just arrived from Donegal, the procession was new to me. Later I found out the tradition of the processions went back centuries to Medieval times and that it was possibly pagan in origin. The procession was held every year at the beginning of May in all the Catholic churches in England and the purpose was to honour Mary, the Virgin Mother. The day usually involved parading around the grounds of the local church, the singing of Marian hymns, and culminated in the statue of Mary being crowned with a wreath of May blossoms by the May Queen.

The playground chatter earlier in the day had been that one girl in my class, Ann O, was the obvious choice for the queen. She was the prettiest and also the most popular. She radiated a degree of confidence beyond her tender years. Not everyone agreed though. Bridget, the class bully, declared. "I think it should be me; she's the teacher's pet. It's not fair if she gets it. "

Nobody said anything, but from what I could gather, we were all praying it wouldn't be her. For if it was, we'd never hear the end of it.

When we were waiting impatiently for the bell to ring for home time. Miss Lynch asked for quiet and continued. "I know that everyone has been waiting to hear about the May procession. You can all be in it, wearing your First Holy Communion costumes, so nobody should be disappointed. This year, I have decided that the May Queen will be Ann O. I'm sure she will make a wonderful queen and not let the school down."

The entire class turned their heads to Ann, who was smiling modestly. Miss Lynch continued, "Ann McFadden, [me] and Margaret M. and John S. are to be the attendants.

Could all the children whose names I've called out stay behind tonight for a few minutes whilst I talk to them about their roles."

When the teacher called out my name, my mind went blank, I had been chosen. Now, as the rest of the class filed out, girls stopped at my desk, congratulating me. I was dumbstruck. Mammy would be so proud. I couldn't imagine why a skinny girl like me, plastered in freckles, could be so lucky. It was hardly on the basis of my looks, which disappointingly didn't seem to be improving with age.

Before long the great day arrived and in the church hall, we changed into our costumes. The room was frantic with teachers busily dashing here and there, pinning girls into dresses, fixing veils in place, checking the bunches of flowers and stopping the children from squabbling.

"Please Miss, Mary keeps standing on my dress," squealed one little girl.

"No I'm not, I just slipped," said the other.

"Will you please stand still and stop fidgeting, while I pin up the end of your dress," snapped Miss Lynch, her temper beginning to fray.

Margaret and I were ready first, the long gowns too big on us and drooping over our skinny frames. I didn't mind, because I had never worn a long dress before. It swished as I walked and I felt like Cinderella going to the ball. However, the headdress was a different matter. It was a blue and white bonnet with what I thought looked like rabbits ears on the top. To my mind, it spoiled my whole look. I had to be persuaded to wear it. Ann O was all serene calm, looking radiant in her May Queen outfit, a long silken white dress, with a bright blue train and in her hands she carried a bunch of spring flowers. John wore a sailor suit with short pressed trousers and he carried a cushion with Our Lady's crown on top.

Our parade began with the singing of "Queen of the

May," and was led by the priest and altar boys. They were followed by several of the men of the parish carrying a slightly old and weather-beaten statue of Our Lady high on a plinth. Next came our small party, then a posse of schoolchildren dressed in their First Communion finery, boys in short trousers and white shirts and girls in dresses pale as icing sugar, glistening in the morning sunshine. Our young voices rang out above the traffic, as we made our way around the shabby streets and into the chapel.

Once we were all inside, the organ belted out "Hail Queen of Heaven" and the Queen's party made its way to the altar. The congregation took their seats in the pews. I turned around just in time to see my mother and my brothers sliding into the seats at the back of the church, whispering and pointing in my direction. The room was crammed full. Over the previous few days, the Catholic Mothers' Union had cleaned and polished every seat and window and the entire altar was festooned with flowers.

I glided to the front, making sure not to stumble or fall over the Queen's train. I was a bag of nerves, but determined to do my part. We sang several hymns, our voices straining above the organ and then we knelt down and said the Rosary. The peak of the proceedings was when the May Queen crowned the statue. We all applauded and the Priest retired to the vestry to prepare for Benediction, the prayers after Mass.

Afterwards, in the church hall, as we feasted on Spam sandwiches and fairy cakes, I sought reassurance.

"Do you think I was all right, Mammy, did I look nice?"

"You looked lovely, Ann, like a princess. I thought you were the best of all."

I smiled, happy that my job was well done.

To my great delight, the press came and took our pictures that afternoon, so next evening I rushed to the shop for the Evening Telegraph. Turning the pages, I found my picture, on page eight. Smiling shyly at the camera, I stood in all my finery, holding the Queen's train. None of my friends had been in the papers. Mammy cut the article out of the newspaper and we put it in our photograph album. It's still there to this day.

Chapter 12 - Friendship

We had settled into our new life in Coventry and most evenings there would be a knock on the back door. "Can Ann come out to play?"

Before Mammy could reply, I had put on my coat, collected my two tennis balls, and was running with Olwen to the entry at the back of our yard.

"Be in before dark," was my Mammy's parting shot as the door slammed behind me. I wasn't listening. I couldn't wait to throw off the constraints of school and get out into the open air. The "entry", through our back gate, was cobbled, and clinging round the edges were old newspapers, beer bottles and cigarette butts. The walls were thick with childish graffiti. "Up with the Sky Blues", "Olwen loves Peter", "Miss Lynch is the devil." This was our domain, mine and my pals; somewhere to play, honing our skills practising "two ball." Day in, day out, every evening, the rubber balls were juggled against the walls: over and back they went, between hand and wall, up and down, back and forth, rat, tat, tat, as we'd chant, "One, two, three O'Leary, four, five, six O'Leary, seven, eight, nine O'Leary, ten O'Leary, catch the ball," and at this point, Olwen would take over. Relentlessly we competed with one another over who was the best, who would make the fewest mistakes. Olwen was always more proficient than me; she'd had more practice and she had a better eye for the ball. But I didn't care. I was captured by the easy charm of my new friend.

When we'd had enough two ball, we usually hung out with a group of kids, boys and girls of all ages, whose parents were Irish. Looking like a tribe of pygmies, we stalked the familiar streets. Playing tig, up and down entries, over walls, across roads, pounding our territory relentlessly. We were rowdy, loud, uncouth, and frequently disturbed the neighbours, especially where the man of the house worked nights. Women shouted at us that we were a disgrace to our parents and needed to be controlled and what would the priest say? In return, we gave plenty of back chat and then vanished before they could clip us round the ear. It was an exhilarating time, one filled with childhood adventures, of friendships and falling out, of rivalries and loyalties. I was passionate about my friend and jealously guarded our friendship, even against my mother, who was always giving out that I spent too much time with my pal. On quiet evenings we strolled arm in arm like two old spinsters, sharing our secrets in conspiratorial whispers.

Occasionally, when Olwen's mum was out and my friend had the place to herself, we would sneak into her front parlour. This was "top secret", as her parents would have killed her if they found out. It was nothing like our front room, which had been commandeered for extra sleeping space. Olwen's was like a pixie cave, full of interesting and precious things. The floor was covered in shiny new linoleum and spread with thick-pile rugs. There was a velvet three-piece suite, with multi-coloured crocheted cushions artfully arranged on it. The room smelled of polish and I could see specks of dust in the air floating all around me. In one corner of the room stood a handsome oak sideboard, with heaps of fine, fragile-looking coloured glass animals, vases and fancy plates, all neatly displayed on the shelves.

Pride of place was given to the pianola, which stood against the dividing wall between our two houses. When I first set eyes on the instrument, I couldn't believe what I was seeing. It looked like a piano, but the keys moved independently, playing a tune all on their own. Olwen would wind it up and then we would listen in reverence to the works of Gershwin and Scott Joplin, whilst relaxing on their Sunday-best settee, gorging ourselves on Dairylea cheese triangles, which she had swiped from her mother's kitchen. These stolen moments never lasted long, for we were always on the lookout for Olwen's mother returning from the shop, or her brother or sister, who would surely tell on us.

Friday nights, our dads' pay-day, was our favourite time of the week. With our threepence pocket money we bought the same thing each week, a packet of cheese crisps and a Milky Way. Perched high up on the wall, like hungry cubs, we feasted on our bounty, squashing the crisp packet between our hands and then making them last an age by eating the particles, one by one. The Milky Way we sucked like a lollipop until it shrunk to a tiny sliver that melted gloriously on our tongues.

One night we were sitting on the wall just finishing our crisps. Some pigeons were scratching around below us, fighting over a few crumbs we had thrown down to them. It had been a lovely day. The sun was going down, the light had turned to a hazy lavender, the hum of traffic had stopped and people were starting to settle down for the night.

Olwen asked, "Do you know where babies come from?"

"They come from the stork, you can pick them up at the hospital. I remember when we got Pat he was tiny and had a bald head." I replied knowledgeably.

"But that's not true," Olwen said. "I found out how they really come. But it's a secret. You won't tell, will you?"

"Cross my heart and hope to die."

Margaret in my class says they come out of our mummies' tummies," she whispered.

"How do they get out then?"

"She told me there's a hole between her legs, where you wee out of, and they just pop out there."

"That's horrible, and dirty, I'm sure that can't be right. When I saw Pat he was nice and clean, he was in a white shawl. He looked like a little Eskimo."

"That's because they cleaned him up, he would have been covered in blood and guts and things."

I shook my head. "No, that can't be true, for if he was dirty like that, then I'm sure my Mammy would have sent him back. She can't abide dirt."

There were many conversations like this, as together we discovered the facts of life and our place in the world. I was friends with Olwen for all the time I was at junior school, but then when I was around twelve, we fell out. I can't remember what prompted the row, but we didn't speak for two years. Although we made it up, the friendship was never the same again. After I left home, we lost touch and I have no idea if she married, had children, or where she lives now.

Childhood relationships can be all-consuming. My friendship with Olwen provided an important distraction from the feelings of bewilderment and loss I experienced when I first arrived from Donegal and helped me to settle into life in the inner city. The awareness of the gloomy streets around me and the damp decaying house we lived in faded into the back ground as our companionship came to mean everything to me.

Olwen taught me important lessons about loyalty, sharing and intimacy. She helped me to think of myself as an independent being, separate from my family, not just a daughter or a sister. On reflection it seems to me that as we grow older, the nature of our friendships change, they become less intense and more relaxed. Although I made lots of friends in my adult life, I never again recaptured that closeness with a friend that I shared with Olwen all those years ago. I think that's the same for most people.

Olwen was there for the next big change in my life. It had been a sweltering hot day and Olwen and I were sitting on the wall making plans for how we would spend the summer holidays. My first year at St Mary's was at an end and I was excited at the prospect of moving up into a higher stream in September. The streets were quiet, the evening light was fading gently and most of our playmates had been called in for the night.

Suddenly Pat shouted from our back door. "Mammy

says you've got to come in and do the dishes. I'm not doing them again. It's your turn."

"I'll be in in a minute."

"You're to come right away," he insisted.

Reluctantly I jumped down from the wall and said goodbye to Olwen.

"What time shall I call for you tomorrow?" Olwen shouted as she disappeared into her back yard.

"About ten. Then I'll ask Mammy if we can go to Gosford Green Park."

As I entered the kitchen I could see the mound of greasy evening dishes waiting for me in the sink. My heart sank. I was in no mood to tackle them, certainly not without a fight.

"I did them last night. It's your turn tonight," I said to Pat.

"But Mammy says you have to do them tonight, because you missed the night before. That makes it your turn again." Pat stuck out his tongue at me.

I wasn't about to agree and so we continued to argue back and forth until we heard a familiar voice from the other room.

"That's enough now. Stop the arguing this minute. Come here, I've something to say to you both."

Pat and I trooped into the living room, heads hung low, ready for a good telling-off.

Mammy was sitting in her chair by the fire, a broad smile on her face. "How would you like to go and stay with Auntie Mary for a while? I've to go into hospital and Auntie Mary said she would love it if you both went to stay."

Pat and I looked at each other and then at Mammy.

"I've to go for a rest, until I'm feeling better," she explained.

"What's wrong with you? Are you sick? Is it your heart?" I added pensively.

"The doctors say I have to take it easy and that's why I thought you'd like to go to Auntie Mary's."

"Why do we have go there? Daddy could look after us," I said indignantly.

"Your daddy's at work. He won't be able to look after you all. Johnjoe, Charlie and Michael will be going to Father Hudson's to stay with the nuns."

Father Hudson's Homes was a large children's home in Coleshill, on the outskirts of Birmingham, run by the Catholic Church. I was familiar with the place mainly because at school, during Lent, we saved up the pennies we didn't spend on sweets and donated them to the Home.

There was a stunned silence as Pat and I tried to take in what she was saying.

"Don't worry, it's not going to be for very long. Daddy will be at home on his own, but he'll be over to see you often. You're to be on your best behaviour. Anne and Eddie are looking forward to having their cousins to visit. And the nuns will take good care of the boys."

Mammy was looking intently at us both, trying to gauge our reaction. For a moment I was lost for words. "Why do we have to leave Daddy. Who'll keep house for him?" I demanded.

"Daddy can look after himself."

This was not the answer I was hoping for. I was in a state of panic and thought quickly. "But I could stay at home and look after everyone. I'm good at cleaning and making the beds. You said I'm like a wee housewife myself. Pat can help and we can get the dinner ready for Daddy when he comes home from work."

Mammy stretched her arms out, drawing Pat and me close to her.

"You know, Auntie Mary would be upset if you don't go. She told me she was really looking forward to having you. And you'll be going to a brand new school."

"But I don't want to go to a new school - I like St Mary's. And what about the boys? Charlie and Michael are only babies, they'll forget all about us, " I pointed out.

Mammy sighed loudly and said sharply, in a firm voice, "Don't make a song and dance about it. This is difficult enough. You and Pat are old enough to understand. We're doing the best we can. Please God we'll all be back together soon."

Mammy had spoken and that usually meant the end of it, but Pat wasn't satisfied. "Why can't I go to Father Hudson's with the others? I could look after them."

"No, Pat, you're to go with Ann. I'm light in the head thinking about it, and I don't want another word."

Pat set his jaws firmly and stamped his feet. "Well, then, why can't the boys come with us to Auntie Mary's?"

"Auntie Mary hasn't room for all of you. She has a business to run. She wouldn't have time to look after the boys."

"But they're too wee to be on their own. Johnjoe's only four and Charlie and Michael are just babies." Said Pat.

Mammy closed her eyes for a moment and when she opened them said "Johnjoe will look after Charlie and Michael. Daddy will visit them every weekend. The nuns will take good care of them. They won't want for anything. They'll be grand. It's not for long. We'll all have to be very brave."

"But Father Hudson's is for orphans. We collect money for them at school." Pat pointed out.

"I know the boys aren't orphans, but the nuns look after other children too," Mammy explained.

The news was just beginning to sink in and I felt numb. It was true that I loved to visit my aunt, but it was another thing altogether going to live with her. I was in a panic. Mammy was going away and we were all having to leave home.

She grasped me by the shoulders, her eyes boring into mine.

"You're the eldest. You're eight years old and I'm relying on you to be sensible, to mind your brother and not be any trouble to Auntie Mary."

It was all too much for Pat, He started to sob, mumbling, "I can look after myself, I'm old enough."

Mammy laughed, and said, "You're not old enough. You're only five. You need someone to mind you. I can't, because I'll be in the hospital and Daddy's at work. Your brothers will need someone to mind them, too, that's why we have to send them to Father Hudson's. You'll see: Anne and Eddie will be good fun to play with. There'll be lots of toys and you can go to the park across the road to play."

"When do we have to go?" I demanded, not far off tears myself.

"Soon. We'll pack your cases tomorrow morning. You can both help. The Sacred Heart will be looking down on us. Everything's going to be fine. We'll be back together in no time at all. Please God. You'll see."

But that was it, I didn't see. I was convinced I could stay home and look after my brothers myself. That night I couldn't get to sleep. I felt afraid and uneasy thoughts raced through my mind. What if I didn't like my new school? What if Olwen found another friend? What if I didn't like it at Auntie Mary's? I tossed and turned, thumping my pillow and worrying more and more about leaving home. Sleep came eventually, long after Mammy and Daddy went to bed, but it was fitful and filled with anxious dreams.

Chapter 13 - Another New Home

The next day, my aunt turned up to collect Pat and me. Before we knew it, we were all standing on the doorstep saying our goodbyes. There were no tears. Such things were frowned on in our house, especially from me, for as the eldest, I had always been encouraged to think of myself as a grown-up. It was just like any other day. Mammy buttoned up my jacket up and handed me our case. "God bless and don't be any trouble to Auntie Mary. Be on your best behaviour. Daddy will be out to see you at the weekend."

Mammy bent down and I put my arms around her neck. She was smiling broadly and in my arms she felt warm and comforting. Her lips brushed the top of my head. I hugged Charlie and Johnjoe as they stood together on the step, clutching Mammy's skirts. Pat shook hands with the two boys. As we walked up the street, I kept turning and Mum and the boys were standing on the step, waving. They stood there until we turned the corner at the top of the road and then disappeared from view.

Travelling on the bus, my few belongings clutched on my knee, I felt anxious and unsure. Auntie Mary tried to reassure me.

"Don't worry sweetheart, your Mammy will be all right, Anne and Eddie are looking forward to having you both to stay. It will be just like home. You'll see."

But I wasn't mollified. I had a sickening feeling in the pit my stomach. I was scared about leaving my family.

"When will I see Mammy and the boys again?" I asked.

"Not for a while yet. Children aren't allowed to visit her in the hospital, but your daddy will come to see you soon."

"Will I be able to see the boys?"

"I'm not sure, Ann. Maybe."

"They'll be frightened. They won't know anyone."

"Don't worry," Auntie Mary said, putting her arm round

my shoulder and squeezing me. "The nuns will take good care of them. They'll settle in, in no time at all."

My aunt's words hung in the air between us. I could see she was trying to comfort me and I felt grateful to her, but anxiety was nibbling away at me. Especially at the prospect of staying with my cousins. I hardly knew them. We had met for the first time only a few months before when they came to live in Coventry from Morley. They were strangers. My mind flashed back to when I was much younger, when Mammy was ill before. I remembered being dragged, screaming, to unfamiliar houses and left there whilst she recovered. At the time I had the distinct impression that I was viewed me as an interloper, an unwelcome guest. What would my English cousins make of me ? I tried not to think about it. All of a sudden a picture of the park across the road from my aunt's flashed before me. It was a great playground, with dozens of swings, a roundabout and slides. With any luck, we could play there every day. I smiled to myself as I imagined the fun I would have. At least there would be some compensation.

Uncle Bill opened the heavy wooden door and, smiling broadly, he took my case as he led us into the large hallway.

"Well, if it isn't our two young guests come to stay with us for a while."

Anne and Eddie were standing behind him peering shyly at us. I smiled lamely across at them. I could tell that Pat felt as awkward as me. For once I was silent. I didn't know what to say, whether to laugh or cry.

"First things first," Auntie Mary chirped, taking our coats and hanging them up. Turning briskly to her children she commanded "Show your cousins where they'll be sleeping."

Anne blushed and indicated she wanted me to follow her. Pat went off with Eddie in the other direction. I followed Anne through the kitchen to a room I had never been to before. In my memory it was small and brightly decorated, with a bed in the corner. I have since learned that the room in fact was quite large and held not only our bed but also the one belonging to my aunt and uncle.

It smelled of polish. Books lay on shelves and toys were piled neatly to one side of the room. No socks or underwear littered the floor; all was neat and tidy. Nothing like the damp, untidy bedroom I shared with my brothers at home. It felt unreal, as if I was dreaming. Up until now, Anne and I had been on nodding terms; we had dutifully played together when we came to visit, but now we were to be bedfellows. Straight away, I panicked that I might wet the bed.

"Mummy says you're to put your clothes in the drawer and when you've unpacked you can put your pyjamas under the pillow." She pointed to the bed we were to share.

As quickly as I could, I fumbled about with my clothes, laid them carefully in the deep drawers, which smelled strongly of camphor, and then folded my pyjamas under the pillow as instructed. Anne put out the light and we made our way into the living room to join the others. I was trembling all over and my confidence had deserted me. I felt close to tears. Auntie Mary pointed to the settee and told me to sit down. A moment later she appeared from the kitchen with a huge plateful of sandwiches and cakes for us all to eat. Everyone was smiling reassuringly, but the atmosphere was strained. I could sense they were all trying hard to make us feel comfortable. Pat came and sat beside me and immediately dived on the sandwiches. I felt a bit better and began to relax and watch TV. Televisions were a novelty at the time: very few people, including us, owned one. Before very long I found myself engrossed in the programme, quite forgetting the painful events of the day.

That night, as I lay in bed beside my cousin, I listened to the patter of the rain on the window and sound of Anne breathing next to me. I felt wide awake and tossed and turned, trying not to disturb her, still worrying about wetting the bed. In the back of my mind, I had an image of my brothers crying for Mammy. I tried to block it out. Mammy said they would be all right, but they were just babies. The thought filled me with horror. I tried to settled down to sleep, but felt overwhelmed with emotion. Anxious tears hovered at the back of my eyes, but I held back. I was the eldest and I wasn't about to show myself up by acting the sissy. As sleep started to claim me, all I could think about was that I was in a strange bed, and my mammy was far away in hospital.

My aunt and her family owned a large boarding house in a leafy, upmarket district of Coventry. They had the ground floor of the house and the lodgers lived above them. Their flat, which was easily the size of our whole house, looked out through a large bay window to tennis courts across the road. Where our home was cramped and dark, this was spacious, with high ceilings and was flooded with light. Here, instead of crumbling lino on the floors and badly mended second-hand chairs, there was a living room with a fitted carpet and highly polished and expensive furniture. An elegant mahogany sideboard graced one side of the room and in front of it, there was an enormous dining table with six matching chairs. Sitting resplendent in the middle of the sideboard was a brass dinner gong, which summoned us to our evening meal.

Unlike life at home, where mealtimes were a staggered, raucous affair, dinners here were formal occasions, when we all sat down together. Elbows were definitely off the table and please and thank you was much in evidence. When we finished we had to say to the grown-ups, "Please may I leave the table, because I've said my grace."

Quite early on, Pat and I realised that manners were important in this home and that we had to be on our best behaviour at all times. We ordinarily fought like cat and dog, but here, we had an unspoken truce, comrades in this unfamiliar landscape, determined not to let our parents down. Here, we learned that we couldn't run wildly about the house, but had to conduct ourselves calmly, we had to say "pardon" and "excuse me" an awful lot, and we had to tidy our things away every night and be careful with our cousins' toys.

To us it seemed that Anne and Eddie had an army of toys: dolls, prams, teddy bears, toy racing cars - things I only dreamed about. My favourite was a farmyard with tiny chickens and pigs and geese, true to life in every way. I begged to be allowed to play with them every chance I could. Toys here were treasured, cared for, not like at home, where they were thrown about carelessly or left lying in the back yard, growing rusty. Here, each toy had its place and was tidied away neatly, ready for the next time it would be taken out and played with. I envied them their possessions, their surroundings. Although we were related, the difference between our two families seemed immense.

Overall my memories of my stay with my aunt are full of warmth and affection. It was a happy household, with much laughter and merriment, especially at meal times. Whatever quantity or type of food that was placed in front of Pat, he devoured it, like Desperate Dan in the *Dandy* comic. One Sunday, as Pat reached for his third helping of roast potatoes, Auntie Mary teased him. "Pat! As far as I can see you must be nearly fit to burst. When do you know you've had enough?"

Pat glanced up, thought for a moment, and with a very serious look on his face said, "When I get a pain."

We all roared with laughter and Pat stared at his plate, blushing to the roots of his hair.

Pat was always full of mischief and often irreverent about our aunt. Soon after we arrived, she bought a new fitted carpet and kept scolding us to "mind the carpet." One day, when she was out of earshot, Pat ran around the house, squealing, "mind the carpet, mind the carpet," at the top of his voice. This soon became his mantra and whenever he was slightly unhappy about anything she said or did, he'd repeat the same phrase over and over behind her back. I doubt if our mother would have approved, but every time he did it, I would collapse in a fit of the giggles.

Auntie Mary was older than Mum. She was a whirling dervish of a woman, always on the go, who had plenty to say and didn't mince her words. She never really thought my father was good enough for my mother and strongly disapproved of his drinking. She didn't hold back, letting him know about her feelings frequently. As I was growing up I heartily approved of this side of Auntie Mary, for to me it seemed there was nobody else to stand up to my dad. All too often it was Auntie Mary who took my mother's side, pleading with Dad to change his behaviour and make her sister's life easier.

She was always a welcome visitor to our house and when she first arrived from Morley, we visited her often for Sunday tea. "Any news?" was their favourite refrain. "News" mostly clattered through the letterbox in the form of bulging envelopes of blue airmail notepaper from sisters, brothers, and cousins in Ireland. Brimming with the latest gossip, such as who was "doing a line" with who, and who had passed away, the letters were eagerly digested and discussed, every word and sentence weighed against the next. Mary was a no-nonsense lady, but she enjoyed a good night out, with an occasional glass of sherry. She was always full of talk of old friends in Morley and the shop she used to keep there with Uncle Bill. Exactly the sort of person to run a busy boarding house, she was bursting with lively conversation, hardly stopping to draw breath. They had moved to Coventry when Uncle Bill landed a job in a local engineering factory and Auntie Mary, always one to spot a business opportunity, had jumped at the chance to buy the boarding house and run it herself.

Popular with her lodgers, she took the young single, homesick Irishmen to her heart, coddling them, caring for them like their own mother. In return, they were happy to do odd jobs around the house. For years, one pair of bachelors from Donegal, Tony and Michael, kept her lawn manicured and roses pruned to perfection. They were tall, rough-looking navvies, but kind and gentle as anything, with a great sense of humour. Apparently Tony, well aware of the importance of their work in the garden, used to joke, "no buds, no bed." They were great friends and remained in contact with my aunt long after they retired back to Donegal.

Uncle Bill was exactly the opposite of his wife. Quiet and reserved in company, preferring to let Auntie Mary do the talking, he often seemed like the power behind the throne. A Yorkshireman through and through, he had a certain stature about him, stern, dependable. With small crinkly eyes, he had a warm smile and loved to tell the same corny stories over and over again. A deeply religious man, he had a special fondness for St Thérèse of Lisieux, whom he credited with keeping him safe during the War. He was a teetotaller and strongly disapproved of drink. Poles apart from my father, unlike my aunt, he never partied with my parents at the Finbarr's, the social club for Irish people in Coventry. Instead, Bill was a home body, his social life was the family and the church. He liked nothing better than to settle down at night, reading the paper or teaching his children.

My cousin Eddie, at eleven, had the usual disdain for younger kids and was often reluctant to play with the rest of us. He was a quiet, tall boy, with a serious expression who loved a game of draughts. I fancied myself as a bit of a player and was forever challenging him, which he reluctantly agreed to now and again, to shut me up, though he didn't always beat me.

Anne, a year younger than me, was more of a playmate and she taught me how to work myself up on the swings without needing to be pushed. I was thrilled to acquire this new skill and couldn't wait to show it off to Olwen. I was very envious of Anne as she had a beautiful tortoiseshell cat named Pixie and every afternoon the cat would wait at the front door for Anne to return home from school. Best of all, my cousin wasn't precious about her toys and was always willing to share. We all regarded Anne as the brainy one amongst us, as she always seemed to have her head in a book. My friendship with her was not like that with Olwen: we weren't bosom pals, but we got along.

Everyone in the household treated me with kindness and consideration. There was no spite or animosity between me or my cousins, but often I felt the difference in our status. For all my young years, I felt keenly that we were the poor relations, lower down the pecking order than they.

Chapter 14 - A Welcome Sight

As the summer wore on, Pat and I spent most of our time across the road playing in the park. It was a great treat to have a playground so close to hand and when I was swinging high over the tree-tops, I forgot all about Mum and my younger brothers and just concentrated on having fun.

One day we were about to go to the park as usual when my aunt announced we were going on a surprise trip. We begged to know where it was, but she wouldn't tell. All she would say was, "Just wait and see." First we caught a bus into town and then another. We recognised this as our route home to Cambridge Street. The sun was blazing down and the heat was beating off the pavements. To cool us down, Auntie Mary had bought us all orange ice lollipops. I was engrossed in sucking mine when she instructed us to get off the bus. I looked up. The surroundings seemed familiar. I noticed Swanswell Park just over the road. Mum and Dad used to take us there as a treat, to play on the swings and to fish for tiddlers. With a cheap fishing net bought from the paper shop around the corner, we spent hours leaning over the walls of Swanswell Pool, searching its muddy interior for those tiny, slippery fish. No matter how carefully we carried them home, we would only see them perish a few days later when they resisted all attempts to feed them with bread.

I imagined for a moment that we were going fishing, but instead we walked over to a collection of modern buildings I had never noticed before. I still had no idea where we were going. I looked at Auntie Mary for some clue. She was saying nothing but seemed in high spirits, pleased with herself. Now, taking our hands, she walked us to the back of the complex, into a courtyard surrounded on all sides by high buildings with lots of windows.

"Wait here, I have something to do, I'll be back in ten minutes," she ordered.

With this she disappeared through a door.

Pat and I just stood there, abandoned and silent. I felt stupid standing around. What were we doing here? Would we be long?

Pat took a ball out of his trouser pocket and started slamming it against the wall.

"Stop that. You'll get into trouble," I reprimanded.

"I'm bored, I want to go home."

I couldn't be bothered arguing with him, so I let him get on with it, and sat down on the edge of the pavement making patterns in the dirt with my shoes. It seemed like ages before Auntie Mary reappeared again and when she did, she pointed to a distant window several floors up.

"Look. Who can you see?" We peered upwards, not knowing what to expect. There, in the distance, we could see someone waving and realised, to our great surprise, that it was our mum. She was shouting down to us and waving like mad. I was elated. Pat and I just screamed at the top of our voices,

"Mum, Mum, we're here."

I could hardly believe that at last I was seeing her again. She was so small and distant, but she was unmistakably my mum. At once, I conjured up the familiar smell of her perfume as she kissed me goodnight, the flick of her hand on my hair as she brushed it in the morning. Most of all, I imagined myself throwing my arms around her waist, pulling her to me, demanding her attention. Now I made do with frantic waving, jumping and shouting till I was hoarse.

"We go to the park every day and play on the swings," I screamed upwards, eager to pass on my news.

"I've learned how to play draughts and I can beat Ann," Pat shouted, he too, not quite believing what was happening.

Mum kept on smiling and waving down to us and it was enough; I could feel the blood pounding round my body with excitement. I hadn't realised till I saw her again, how much I missed her, how much we both missed her.

We spent about an hour there, calling and shouting, before my aunt pulled Pat and me towards the bus stop, telling us it was time for home.

"Well, was that a good surprise," my aunt beamed as we all sat together on the journey home.

"That was the best present ever. When can we see her again?" I demanded, unwilling to let this be a one-off.

"Well in a few weeks, but we mustn't tire her out, the doctors say she needs to rest." I didn't care, my mum was back in my life. I had seen her, she was safe and now I felt confident that she would soon be returned to us.

As the months slipped by, we fell into a familiar routine. Dad would visit us and occasionally we would go the hospital yard to visit Mum. However, during the nine or ten months we spent away from home, I never once visited my younger brothers.

Of course, we heard about them: Dad would give us news and often bring pictures of matchstick families they'd drawn for us as presents. At night, lying in bed next to my cousin, I would try to picture "the home." In my mind's eye, I imagined vast dormitories of cots, with nuns patrolling, and babies crying for their mothers, stretching out their arms to be picked up. Dad assured us Johnjoe was like "a little mother" to Charlie and Mick. He said they were always together. I prayed that was true. But, I wondered, what did they remember of the rest of us? Were we just a distant memory that had we just faded into the past?

It's always likely to be traumatic when families are ripped apart, regardless of the reason or the circumstances. But Pat and I were fortunate. They were anxious times for both of us, but we were with a loving family whom we knew and trusted. It must have been a thousand times worse for my little brothers. They were all under five, too young to really understand what was going on. In the course of writing this memoir I asked my brothers if they had any memory at all of how they felt at the time. No-one did, because they were so young, but on reflection, they must have thought they'd been abandoned altogether.

As the summer came to an end and there was no word of us going home, Pat and I were enrolled at a new school. Every morning we all caught the bus to school, me, Pat and Anne to All Souls Primary School and Eddie to the secondary one. Anne was entrusted with the fares, which I felt slightly aggrieved about, as I was the eldest. Unlike St Mary's, All Souls was an old brick building, with shabby looking classrooms facing out onto the playground. Draughty and cold, the rooms had none of the cheeriness I had become accustomed to at St Mary's. Worst of all, the toilets were dark, smelly and dirty. I dreaded every trip to their sinister interior, fearing that one day I would be locked inside. At this school I was bewildered, I didn't understand the lessons and still struggled with my reading. I felt ashamed as Anne was far more advanced than me, even though she was a year younger.

I don't know how it came about, perhaps the school said something, but Uncle Bill noticed my problems with reading and to my utter dismay, decided he would try and help. So night after night, instead of heading to the park with Anne and Pat, we sat down together and he made me read Rupert Bear books aloud.

These stories, which were very popular at the time, were about the adventures of a teddy bear who wore yellow checked trousers. He had all sorts of exciting and interesting mishaps with a bunch of friends. I always enjoyed looking at the pictures and could make out most of the meaning of the captions, but Uncle Bill insisted I read them out to him. Mostly, I stumbled on my words, frantically searching for clues to what the jumble of letters meant. As I painfully sounded out my words, resentment bubbled up in me against Uncle Bill and I grew to hate Rupert Bear. It was a couple of years later when I eventually learned to read. I was ten and a group of us had been singled out for special tuition by a student teacher. With patience and sensitivity, the young man gradually taught me to sound out my letters and pick up the words from there. Although my experience with Uncle Bill had been troubling I don't doubt the grounding he gave me went a long way towards my mastering this essential skill, and held me in good stead when I went to secondary school. It was only as an adult with children of my own that I began to appreciate the care and attention he had bestowed on me.

Chapter 15 - Visiting Home

It was nearly Christmas and Pat and I hadn't been back home to Cambridge Street for six months. I missed it and I was desperately homesick. I was forever badgering my aunt to take me back there, just to see my old home and to play with Olwen again. Eventually she relented and we three headed off. I was bursting with anticipation and excitement as we knocked at the front door. Dad answered and seemed delighted to see us. But as we went inside, I could sense that the house was different. My mother wouldn't have recognised it. It felt empty and cold And the furniture had been rearranged. Every surface was covered in dirty clothes, newspapers or rubbish. It smelled different too, reeking of smoke and stale alcohol. Half-empty beer bottles were thrown into a corner. In the kitchen, unwashed dishes, covered in grease, lay in piles in the sink. It seemed the only thing that was the same was the Sacred Heart picture on the wall, with the lamp shining underneath it.

We were all appalled. My aunt didn't hold back. "What's got into you, James? The place is a shambles. What can you be thinking of? What would Nora say if she could see it? Thank God she can't."

Dad hung his head with shame and murmured under his breath. "Well, haven't I enough on my plate with Nora in the hospital and the wains in a home."

But Auntie Mary wasn't about to excuse him. "That's not the point. Nora has standards. She wouldn't be too pleased to see her house like this. Don't you care about your home anymore?"

She was right. It seemed to me Dad didn't care, he wasn't minding the house at all. I felt ashamed of him. To make matters worse, there were unfamiliar clothes and shoes scattered about. It was clear somebody else was staying. I felt horrified.

"Who's living here?" I demanded.

"One of my ol' pals from the Rosses, Seamus Kelly," Daddy replied. "He needed somewhere to kip for a few weeks. The rent has come in handy."

My aunt cast her eyes heavenward then looked at me and Pat.

"And what are the wains supposed to think. Their home being turned upside down by some lodger you've brought in?"

I couldn't have agreed more. A stranger at the very heart of our lives. He was in our house, sitting on our furniture and drinking from our cups. I felt annoyed that my dad would allow such a thing.

"Well, whatever he calls himself, he'd do well to clean up. He's treating this place like an old doss house and you're not helping, James."

Dad pursed his lips, looking distinctly uncomfortable.

"I know it's not a palace, Mary-Ellen, but I'm doing the best I can."

Auntie Mary wagged her finger angrily at Dad.

"We can't leave this place knowing the state it's in."

She turned to me first.

"Open the window and let in a bit of fresh air and then get the broom from the kitchen."

Over the next couple of hours we dusted, polished, tackled the mountain of dishes and swept the floor. We dug out the beer bottles and fag packets from under the settee and consigned them to the dustbin. Before long, the ornaments were set on the mantelpiece, the table was polished and the clothes put away in the wardrobe. When all was done and the house was nice and tidy, I glanced across at Dad. He was sitting in his chair, smoking, his left hand twisting a remaining stray hair on his almost bald head, a nervous trait which is still fondly remembered by all the family. He looked deeply embarrassed, but when he saw me studying him, his mouth suddenly turned into a grin and he beckoned me over.

"How are you getting on at your new school?"

I lied. "I'm doing well, and have loads of gold stars on my schoolbook."

"Your Mammy would be very pleased about that. I'll tell her when I see her tomorrow."

I smiled, delighted at the mention of my mother.

"When will she be coming out of the hospital? Will it be soon?" I asked.

"Soon enough, but for now you've to be good and stay with Auntie Mary. Your daddy misses you all and Mammy misses you too. You're growing into a fine girl, Ann. You're the spitting image of your mother, isn't she Mary-Ellen? Here, sit on my knee while I have a wee chat with your Aunt."

For the next half hour I sat contentedly on Dad's lap while they talked. I was all ears, hoping to pick up any information about Mum. More than anything, I wanted to come home, but not without Mum. The house felt empty without her and the boys.

At the end of the visit Dad came to the door to see us off. He patted Pat and me on the head. "Make your mammy proud. Be good and don't be causing any trouble."

With a heavy heart I walked back up the street, leaving Dad standing alone on the doorstep. I felt miserable to be leaving him, but was relieved to be going back to the familiarity of my aunt's. My house didn't feel like home any more. I realised I didn't feel the same attachment to it without Mum and my little brothers. Instead, I felt alone and confused and longed for us all to be back together.

I suppose I also felt annoyed with Dad, but not surprised. Since I could remember, Mum had been moaning about my father and his shortcomings: his drinking, his willingness to fritter away meagre funds needlessly. This latest incident was just one more thing. I felt ashamed and asked myself why Dad couldn't be more like Uncle Bill. Now, as an adult, I think back to my eight-year-old self and feel I was rather harsh in my judgement. Dad was alone, he was out all day at work. In those days, the lines between the sexes were clearly drawn. It probably would never have occurred to Dad to tidy the place up: he would have seen it as my mother's domain.

There was probably another reason for Dad's disarray on the day we visited, the shock and worry when he realised that Mammy was expecting not one baby, but two. Auntie Mary only recently told me this, recounting the night Daddy came to see her to tell her the news.

As she opened the front door, Mary saw immediately that something was wrong. "What in God's name's the matter with you, James?" she said. "You look as if you've seen a ghost."

"I've just come from the hospital after seeing Nora." Daddy shuffled uneasily from foot to foot.

Now my aunt was becoming concerned. "Come in out of the cold. I'll take your coat. What is it, James? Is Nora all right?"

He handed her his coat and he turned his long thin face towards her, wearing a worried look.

"They say she's expecting twins."

"Thanks be to God. Isn't that lovely, two little babies instead of one."

My aunt patted him on the back.

He relaxed for a moment and smiled. "Hardly believe it myself. I'm blowed if I ever heard tell of twins in the family. Have you?"

"Not on the Boyle's side," Mary said.

He hesitated for a moment, then grabbed my aunt by the arm and locked his eyes on hers. "What'll we do with two more wains, Mary Ellen? How can we feed and clothe them?"

She glanced up at him, paused, and quipped, "You should have thought of that the night you did the damage."

He laughed for a moment, then frowned and said, "What will Nora say?"

"You mean, she doesn't know?" Auntie Mary was incredulous.

"No, the doctors wanted me to tell her, but I couldn't. It'll worry the living daylights out of her. They say she'll be lucky to get through it."

"Oh, James. For the love of God, come and sit down by the fire and I'll get you a glass of whiskey. You look as if you could do with it."

A few whiskies later, Dad turned to my aunt a pained expression on his face. "It would be better coming from you."

"What do you mean, James?"

"I mean, you could tell her. She'd take it better from you," he suggested.

"But you're her husband. You have to tell her," Aunt Mary replied.

"You're her sister. You'd know what to say. How to break it gently."

And, she told me, that's what she did.

The cold, bleak months wore on, until one evening, Eddie and I were sitting in front of a blazing fire, playing draughts. I had taken his last piece to win the game when Auntie Mary called Pat and me over to the settee and asked us to sit down. She was grinning broadly. "Well, haven't I a nice surprise for you. You have two new baby sisters. Twins."

I was amazed and delighted. I had no inkling my mum was expecting a baby, let alone two and I'd never heard of anyone having twins before. That was exotic. I couldn't quite believe it. Pat jumped up from his seat and started running round the room, shouting at the top of his voice, "Yippee, twins, we've got twins." I felt like joining in, too, but dismissed the idea as childish. Instead all I could think of was the pleasure of telling Olwen. She would be so jealous.

In the past I had longed for sisters instead of the procession of boys my mum brought home from the hospital. At eight years old, I thought boys were a damn nuisance. They played too rough and were always fighting. To my mind, girls were far superior.

"When can we see them?" I queried.

"Not at the minute. Mammy's poorly still, but she should be home after Christmas. You can see the babies then."

"What are they called?" Pat asked.

"They haven't got a name yet. Mammy thought you and Pat might like to think of one. They're gorgeous. One has lots of dark hair and thick eyelashes and the other is smaller and dainty with a sweet little bald head."

I adored babies. They were far better than dolls. They smiled and giggled and stopped crying when you picked them up. I could feed them bottles and help bathe them. I couldn't wait to meet them.

Over the next few weeks, as we made preparations to celebrate Christmas, I filled my time with trying to think of suitable names for my little sisters. Ursula and Vanessa were at the top of the long list I sent to Mum in the hospital. I was disappointed when I heard they were to be called Carol and Mary. Far too plain for my liking.

Christmas passed in a haze of pleasure and delight. I remember I got a nurse's outfit and pestered everyone, feeling foreheads and taking temperatures. I was greatly relieved not to have to return to All Souls' school and couldn't wait to get home to meet the youngest additions to the family.

Many years later Mum told me that when the my sisters were delivered safely, they became minor celebrities in the hospital. No-one expected all three to survive and when they did, it was a cause for celebration. She received dozens of cards and bunches of flowers from people she hardly knew and the staff arranged for 'Twenty Tiny Fingers', a popular song at the time, to be played on hospital radio.

It went:

> *"One looks like Mummy with a cute little curl on top*
> *And the other ones got a big bald spot*
> *Exactly like its pop."*

There were to be no more babies for my mother. When I was older, Mum once confided in me, "Your dad only had to shake his trousers at me and I fell pregnant." But following this latest pregnancy, the doctors were emphatic that she would never survive another. In fact, they were appalled that, given her heart condition, she had gone on to have a large family at all. In Ireland, it had been a different story. There, contraception had been outlawed and women were encouraged to have big families, whatever the consequences.

Although she complied with the doctors' advice, Mum was bitterly disappointed that she couldn't have any more children. She told me often she never felt so well, as when she was expecting. As far as she was concerned, she would have loved to have half-a-dozen more. We might have been in England at the start of the Swinging Sixties, but in every way, Mum was the typical long-suffering Irish mammy of days gone by. Living in poverty, rearing a large family and tied to a man overly fond of the bottle, children were her salvation. They gave her a reason to exist, to carry on, they were the lifeblood of her.

Chapter 16 - A Family Reunited

At long last, we were going home. The ground was covered in a white blanket, which stretched out across the park and down the avenue. The streetlights seemed to be wrapped in cotton wool and the buses, as they passed the door, were like giant sheep crawling down the road. I ran outside. The snow crunched under my feet. The plants were drooping with the weight of the snowflakes. Pat and I wanted to build a snowman, but Auntie Mary said we couldn't because we needed to set off before it became too heavy. Instead we gathered our things together and stood waiting for the bus.

It was growing colder and colder, so we tried flapping our arms and jumping up and down trying to keep warm. All the traffic on the roads had slowed down, and the bus was late. When it eventually arrived, there was standing-room only. It took ages to reach town and there it was a different story, the snowfall was hardly settling at all. The force of the traffic had cleared it into a soft slush. I was disappointed, I hoped it would snow forever.

We squeezed onto the 21 bus to Cambridge Street and in the end, we nearly missed our stop, as the conductor only saw us at the last minute. At the top of our road we stood for a moment, looking down. The snow was sparkling in the sunlight, it looked like the street had been sprinkled with a thin layer of icing sugar. All around children were running and skidding in the snow, pulling each other on sledges and people were standing on doorsteps just gazing at the scene.

The road was quiet except for a few buses slipping and sliding around the corners as they made their way back to the depot. The snowflakes were sticking to my eyelashes and covering the top of my coat with a layer of white powder. I was bursting with anticipation. It seemed like a good omen. As Pat and I galloped towards Keppel Street, Auntie Mary shouted, "Remember to look right and left."

We could see Mum at the doorstep, waving and calling to us to mind the road. We crossed over and ran straight into her arms.

"Look how you've grown," Mum declared as she held me at arms' length, "And Pat, you'll soon be as tall as Daddy. I can't believe it."

"Yes, but I'm still the eldest," I said.

"Come inside and meet your two lovely new sisters."

In the living room Mum proudly led us to the large pram, where my two sleeping sisters lay together, heads and tails. I peered in. They were tiny, much smaller even than I'd imagined and they were snuggled underneath a thick layer of baby blankets. They looked so peaceful and contented.

"Can I hold one?" I asked.

"Yes, but be very careful and support her head," Mammy said.

She reached into the pram, plucking one of the sleeping babies from her cosy nest and passed her to me; the other one, she handed to Pat. She was soft like a little kitten and had a warm milky smell. I sat down and examined her. With a small snub nose and a tiny mouth with thin white lips, her hands and feet were hardly the size of a sixpence and she had no hair. I thought she looked like a painting of the baby Jesus, perfect in every way. Suddenly she opened her eyes and glanced up at me, yawned, closed them again and promptly fell asleep. That was enough for me. I was captivated.

"Which one is she?"

"That's Mary. After the Blessed Virgin."

"Can I take them for a walk?" I said, eager to show my sisters off to Olwen.

"When the weather mends and the sun's shining."

After a while Pat and I were reluctantly persuaded to part with our tiny bundles. Pat placed a wriggling Carol back in the pram first. She was waving her tiny arms and legs about, trying to get up. She had a round face, with a mop of dark hair and dark eyelashes. I couldn't believe it when I slipped Mary into the pram opposite her. They were nothing like each other. I'd expected them to be identical.

I was engrossed in studying them both when Pat exclaimed rather loudly.

"We've got a TV!"

I looked up and there, in the corner, was the magic box I'd become so attached to at Auntie Mary's. I never dreamt that we'd ever have one too.

"Can I turn it on?" Pat pleaded.

"There's nothing on at this time of day. The programmes don't start till five o'clock," Mammy said.

But Pat couldn't wait and eagerly pressed the button. After a few minutes the familiar test card appeared. He looked disappointed.

"Time enough for the television. We can all watch it later," Mum said, going up and turning the TV off again.

I was overjoyed and ran to my mother, throwing my arms around her neck.

"This is great, the best homecoming we could ever have." But then stopped for a moment and realised I hadn't seen my younger brothers.

"Where are the boys? Are they here?

"No. Not yet. The nuns want them to stay a while longer. We're having the home help in. I have to take it easy."

I felt disappointed not to see them and asked when they would be home.

"We all have to be very patient. We'll see them soon enough. Now, be a good girl, Ann, and go and put the kettle on and make a nice cup of tea for Auntie Mary. We'll all sit here and you can tell me about what you've been doing since I was in hospital."

I was over the moon. It seemed that at last my family were returned to me. Whilst I adored my aunt and her lovely home, I was relieved to be back with my own parents. Now, it didn't seem to matter that the house was small and poky, that the wallpaper was peeling off the walls with dampness, or that we no longer had a fine garden to play in. Having Mum back in my life was compensation enough.

I don't remember that my relationship with my mother became in any way distant following our separation, rather, it became more intense. Now, I was terrified of losing her again and so redoubled my efforts to please her. My main concern being that if my mother had to go into hospital another time, she might never return. The prospect of her death was a constant and abiding fear throughout my childhood. I worried about it constantly. I can remember lots of occasions travelling home from school, and galloping down Cambridge Street, desperate to assure myself she was still sitting there, in her favourite chair by the fire, knitting.

On a more positive note, I developed a bond with Auntie Mary that has lasted till she passed away in 2013. I can remember on several occasions, when a crisis emerged at home, picking up the phone and seeking her advice. She was always there, full of optimism and practical solutions. Throughout my childhood and adulthood I kept in regular contact with her. At work, my colleagues would tease me as I headed off religiously every Thursday for my bacon sandwich with her. When I moved to Ireland we spoke frequently on the telephone and every time I visited England, she was one of my first stops. Auntie Mary was the last of my mother's family to die. Her death seemed like the passing of an era. She is sadly missed, she meant a great deal to me. She was 96 when she died and thankfully spent all but the last two weeks of her life in her own home and that's no mean achievement. When I think of her it's always with a smile. We had a standing joke between us, when I would ask her how she was getting on. "Struggling on" she would reply and I could tell, even on the telephone that she had a widest grin on her face.

The days waiting for my brothers' return seemed endless, even longer than the school holidays. I thought back to the summer, when I had last seen them standing on the step, waving goodbye. They were so young when they'd gone to the home, I wondered what they would remember of their family and whether they'd recognise us all again, Michael was now just over two years old, Charlie was just three and Johnjoe was coming up to five.

Many years later, my mother told me that the decision to send my brothers to Father Hudson's Homes had been one of the hardest in her life. Sadly, she had no option. Dad had to work and Auntie Mary couldn't have taken us all in. Social Services had wanted the boys to go to foster homes, but at the time there were reports in the press of abuse by foster parents. My parents thought long and hard and eventually decided a Catholic orphanage would be the safest place for them.

At last the day arrived when the boys were expected home. Dad was collecting them and was up much earlier than usual for the long journey by train to the home. He dressed carefully in his best dark grey suit, a heavy black overcoat and a trilby hat. The morning was crisp and clear, with the sky bright blue, and a cold nip in the air. It could have been a spring morning, but for the coldness about the place.

The streets were deserted except for a sprinkling of early shoppers on their way to town, wrapped up in coats and scarves against the winter chill. We waved goodbye and before we knew it, he had disappeared round the corner to catch the bus. Now time dragged endlessly. After a while, we started to slip in and out to the front door, watching anxiously up and down the street for any sign of them.

"When will they be here?"

"They're late now, Mum," Pat and I chanted in turn, as the strain of waiting was telling on us. The day wore on. We had our lunch, then three o'clock came and went and still they had not appeared. It was growing dark and I was starting to worry.

"Do you think something's happened to them? Maybe

they're sick and can't come home." I searched my mother's face for reassurance.

She smiled at me. "They'll be here soon enough. A watched kettle never boils. Here, help me unwind some wool from this hank."

So I stood impatiently, arms aloft, whilst she hummed gently, unwinding the flecked wool. I couldn't understand why she was so calm. Another long hour passed. I looked at the clock again. Half-past four. At long last, there was rattle at the front door. We all leapt up and ran outside. Dad was climbing out of a green car. He had Michael in his arms and a man was letting Johnjoe and Charlie out of the back seat. Seconds later, the car sped off, leaving us all standing, speechless, staring at one another at the front door.

Dad was the first to speak. "Isn't it grand to be home. Look, boys, Mammy and Ann and Pat are waiting here for us."

We stood, frozen like statues, on the doorstep, not daring to move. Suddenly Mum jumped down off the step and snatched Michael from Dad's arms, hugging him close to her chest, burying her head in his small body. Unimpressed by this gesture of ownership, Michael began to scream and in a second, monster tears appeared in his eyes, running down his cheeks, his whole being convulsed in sobs. He turned away from Mum, frantically searching for a familiar face and holding out his chubby arms to be rescued.

"It's all right, Michael. You're with your mammy now. You're home," Mammy explained.

Michael wasn't convinced and continued to screech at the top of his voice. Mum turned to Dad, tears streaming down her face. "He doesn't know me, James. My own son doesn't know me."

"Ah, Nora, he's tired. Here," Dad said and shoved a dummy from his pocket into Michael's mouth.

Mammy said, "All right then, but let's not stand on the doorstep, with all the neighbours gawping at us."

The boys were burying their heads in the folds of Dad's overcoat, unwilling to move. Dad took them by the hand and led them inside. They were wrapped up tight against the cold, like three Egyptian mummies, and stood silent as I peeled off their coats and scarves. They'd grown in the months since I last saw them; they seemed different. Charlie was taller than I remembered, thinner, and Johnjoe had lost weight too. Once their coats were off, they ran over to Dad and attached themselves to his legs, shyly peering at the rest of us. Michael was still bawling loudly, refusing all attempts to pacify him. This couldn't be right, I had imagined their homecoming as spontaneous, joyous, full of celebration, but instead it all felt very fraught and uncomfortable. Johnjoe and Charlie looked uncertain, close to tears.

"Wouldn't shut up in the car, they couldn't wait to get home," Daddy said. "Now the cat's got their tongue. Say something boys. Say hello to your mammy."

The boys glanced at one another and then at my mother. Charlie started to cry and Johnjoe stared down at his feet.

"Jesus, Mary and Joseph, don't you know me, boys, don't you know your mammy?" Mum handed Michael back to Dad and walked towards the two boys, arms outstretched.

Suddenly, Johnjoe let go of Dad's leg and made a dart for Mum. She bent over and he placed his arms around her neck. She hugged him tight, whispering and stroking his hair. My heart was pounding in my chest; tears started to trickle down my face. Mum was laughing and crying all at the same time. Pat and I joined in, the relief and excitement of it all finding a release. Johnjoe was grinning and snuggling up close to Mum, getting as much mileage from his homecoming as possible, savouring the moment.

Now he was speaking nineteen to the dozen. "We had toys to play with. But I didn't like the nuns. They were wil' cross. I even got smacked when I did nothing wrong."

"I'm sure the nuns meant well. You're all grown up, Johnjoe, quite the young man now. What's it like to be home?" Mammy asked.

"This house is so wee. But I don't want to go back there," Johnjoe replied.

Charlie's tiny face was still peering out from behind my Dad's leg.

"Daddy, Daddy", he screamed throwing his hands in the air, wanting to be picked up.

Pat and I glanced at each other, then at Mum. She looked anxious. I went over to Charlie and knelt down beside him.

"Don't you know your mammy, Charlie. You were Mammy's best boy. You've come home haven't you?"

Charlie refused to look at me and cried all the more. His eyes were frantically searching around the room, trying to take in the unfamiliar surroundings. I put my arms around him, he shook me off, but suddenly stopped crying and murmured,

"Want Mammy." Mum reached down and scooped him up, showering kisses all over him, the top of his head, his neck, his spindly arms. It was all too much for Charlie though, he started to cry again, this time more urgently shouting, "Daddy" at the top of his voice.

"My wee Charlie, Mammy's boy Charlie." Mum cradled him in her arms, refusing to let him go.

Johnjoe ran over to him and took his little hand.

"It's all right, Charlie, we're home with Mammy and Daddy now. No need to be upset. You're home."

This seemed to calm him down and he let himself be nursed on my mum's knee. She tickled him, singing his favourite nursery rhyme:

"Charlie Barley butter and eggs,
Sold his wife for two duck eggs
The eggs were rotten, good for nothing
Charlie Barley, butter and eggs."

Charlie chuckled and laughed as Mum jiggled him up and down on her lap. Abruptly the mood in the room lifted. We all looked at each other and smiled. I knew it was going to be all right. Pat ran over and picked Charlie up from Mum's knee and threw him in the air. He screamed in delight. Dad was standing looking across at us.

"Well, I'll be damned," he said, smiling and chuckling to himself as he cradled a sleeping Michael in his arms.

It was at that moment that I remembered Mary and Carol, who had been sound asleep in their pram.

"Johnjoe, do you want to see the twins?"

Johnjoe came over and gazed down at them.

"I've never seen twins before. Do they really belong to us?"

"Yes, we can keep them both, but we have to be very careful with them."

"Can I hold one?" he asked.

"Not yet, you're not old enough. You might drop her," I explained.

"I wouldn't. Cross my heart and hope to die."

"All right then. You sit down on the settee and I'll bring one over." Carefully I scooped my sister Mary up from her pram and placed her gently on Johnjoe's knee. He looked down at her and grinned.

"She's so wee. I'm glad we have two instead of one."

When we were all reunited in that winter of 1961, my parents began the slow process of knitting the family back together again. Every one of us was troubled by the separation but perhaps the youngest, Charlie and Michael, were affected most. They were both under three when the family was split up, and would have had no understanding of what had happened to them. It took a long time for Michael to accept my mother again: he'd had no contact with her for half of his life, and at first, he rejected her outright. Instead he clung stoically to Dad, who had been visiting him on a regular basis.

Thereafter, he was he was always Daddy's boy.

Charlie, on the other hand, reacted totally differently. For years afterwards, he was reluctant to let Mum out of his sight, even for a second. Although Johnjoe had been the only one of them with some sense of what was going on, undoubtedly those long months of separation and uncertainty left psychological scars on him, too.

Mum now had four children, all under five, at home full-time; only Pat, Johnjoe and I were at school. It must have been very trying for her, feeling unwell and constantly trying to reassure anxious toddlers that they wouldn't be shipped off again to a strange place. According to Johnjoe, the family hadn't even been kept together in the orphanage, but had been boarded in separate dormitories. It meant that when the boys eventually returned home, they had the dual challenge of getting to know each other again, as well as the rest of the family. Mum and Dad never talked much about those times, instead they always seemed determined to try and consign them to the past. I guess that when it was all over, Mum must have been exhausted, but immensely relieved to be alive and to have her family back together again. It's frightening to realise that if she had died, most probably Pat and I would have been raised by my aunt, my brothers would have grown up in an orphanage and it's more than likely that my father would have drunk himself to death.

Our family was not unique in skirting tragedy. Economic and other circumstances forced many families to split up at this time and children were either taken into care or farmed out to relatives. When I think of it of it now, I tremble at the close shave we had all those years ago, when circumstances were such we very nearly lost each other. What if it hadn't happened, if Mammy hadn't gone into hospital for those long months. Would we have been a different family to the one we are today? I sometimes wonder. Who can be certain what effect a particular set of circumstances can have, if they

123

change things for better or worse?

Clearly one consequence of the separation could have been the fracturing of family relationships altogether, with my younger brothers feeling rejected and refusing to bond with the rest of the family, or Pat and I, having spent nine months with my aunt and uncle, refusing to accept our parents' authority. Being together again wasn't easy: there were temper tantrums, problems with habitual bed-wetting, rivalries and jealousies, but overall, we were all so relieved to be back home, that we just got on with our lives, as best we could.

I believe that my family shares the same attributes as other large families. We don't live in each other's pockets, but we do try to get together at least once a year, at Christmas, though as circumstances change and children grow older, it becomes more difficult to get everyone in the same place at one time. When we do get together, we tend to stick firmly to each other. When my husband, Charlie, and I threw a party for our 30th wedding anniversary, all my brothers and sisters sat together on the settee all night, chatting to each other, blatantly ignoring everyone else in the room. Even the "the outlaws" complain that after years of marriage, they can't break into our exclusive family club.

Some familial ties are closer than others, though. I text my sisters almost daily, but would only make contact with my brothers every few months. As expected, the twins share the strongest bond of all. And even though now everybody is over fifty, there is still a residue of that past time. I'm still the big sister, the twins are the babies of the family, and Johnjoe still tends to keep a watching brief on Charlie and Michael. And what about the impact on me? Whilst on the surface I seemed fine, what I do know is that after Mammy's departure to hospital, I understood that bad things could happen to my loved ones. I don't remember having a sense of that before. There are plenty of books written about the impact of attachment and loss on mental health and I'm not sure if the seeds of my problems were sewn at that time. It had been a great upheaval and following on the heels of the move to Coventry less than a year earlier, I felt bewildered. Within a matter of hours my family had been flung apart with no sense of when, or if, we'd ever come together again. I was shaken to my core and left with a fear that something worse than even this might be lurking around the corner.

Chapter 17 - Struggling On

After my mother's return, I never really lost that sense of foreboding, the fear that at any moment, she might be taken from me. So, even though the addition of two new babies had brightened all our lives considerably, the strain of the pregnancy had taken a huge toll on my mammy's health. Often I would come home from school to find her collapsed in her chair, her hand to her chest, gasping for breath.

"It's just a dizzy spell. I'll be all right in a minute," she'd protest. I would fret that I might lose her again and offer to get the tea ready or take my sisters for a walk.

Sometimes it was more serious, and Mum would take to her bed. Then Dad, demented with worry, would first call the doctor, and then the priest. Downstairs we would all gather round, not daring to breathe, as upstairs the last rites, the prayers said for the dying, were administered to Mum. If this did no good and she was still in a state of agitation, my aunts would be called to try and calm her down. They would arrive, full of reassurances, and climb the stairs to the sick room where they would spend hours trying to convince Mum that she wasn't about to die. Over the years I've often thought about whether mum was really as ill as she thought, or was having panic attacks caused by general anxiety and depression. Certainly that's the impression I felt her sisters had all those years ago. I don't know the answer, but when she passed away in 1982 at only 59, her worn out heart split open on the operating table, it seemed to suggest she'd been right all along, and that for much of my childhood she had indeed been hovering on the edge of life and death.

These painful episodes were a regular feature of my childhood and we all lived with the constant fear that any minute our mother might be taken from us for ever.

Mum's poor health impacted on the whole family. As

the eldest, I was routinely kept out of school to help with my brothers and sisters and to do the housework, especially after Mary and Carol were born. This happened mainly on Mondays, our wash day. I loathed wash day. Looking back, it always seemed to be icy and cold; I don't remember many sunny wash days, but there must have been some. On those days, Mum and I would gather up a mountain of smelly nappies, sheets, towels and underwear from the bedrooms and stack them in a huge pile in the kitchen.

Most people in the UK and Ireland today have automatic washing machines, but when I was young, a washing machine was considered a luxury. Up to the time Mary and Carol were born, the laundry was done by hand, but then with the need to maintain a supply of clean nappies, my parents decided to invest in a machine on hire purchase. Ours had a large paddle and we filled it from the top with hot water boiled on the gas stove. It was a comforting sound, to hear it chugging away in the kitchen, beating the clothes. When the clothes were done, Mum would fish them out and together we would force them through the wringer at the top of the machine, her pushing and me pulling.

After that, it was my responsibility to hang the washing on the line. It wasn't so bad in the summer but in the winter with freezing hands and knuckles red raw, it was a long painful procedure. Washday usually took all morning and when it was done, Mum would need to lie down for a rest.

One thing that kept my mother going through these difficult times was the Church and I am in no doubt that without it, she would have gone under.

On the occasions when it all became too much, she would leave the house, telling no-one where she was going. Pat and I would panic and run round the streets frantically searching everywhere for her, thinking she'd left for good, only for her to re-appear a couple of hours later, saying she'd been to see the priest. I don't know what comfort or guidance she got, but she would come back replenished, ready to continue with her life.

She was especially fond of doing the "Stations of the Cross." The Stations at St Mary's were a series of engravings arranged around the walls, depicting Christ's journey with the cross, and at each one she would stop and pray. I know these moments alone provided much-needed respite for her, away from clamouring, demanding children. Just saying her prayers became a sanctuary in a very real sense.

With Mum's poor health she turned increasingly to me for help with the latest members of the family. Although it was irksome, I adored my two baby sisters and treated them like my dolls. I loved that they were so small and dainty, their tiny fingers curled round mine as I'd bathed them in the sink and dressed them again. I gave them their bottles, winded them, got them dressed in the morning, took them for walks, entertained them and delighted in encouraging them to take their first steps. Carol was the more adventurous of the two and was always getting into scrapes.

One day, when she was just a toddler playing in the backyard, one of the boys noticed Carol was gasping for breath. Quick as a flash we ran for Mum, who grabbed her, thumping her wildly on the back. It didn't work: she was turning blue and growing limp. As a last resort, Mum prised her mouth open and with her fingers pulled out a marble.

Mary was quieter and was Daddy's girl. He always maintained she was the spit of him, with her long, thin face and light blue eyes. Mary, too, had her fair share of drama when as a small child, she was nearly blinded by a firework in the street. She screamed in pain and had to be rushed to the hospital for emergency treatment. All the family gathered round in shock, waiting anxiously for hours to know if she would be permanently scarred or worse, lose her sight. It was a great relief when Mum returned from hospital with the news that no permanent damage had been done.

When they were a little older and in pushchairs, I made a habit of taking the girls on a Sunday-afternoon walk into the centre of Coventry, around Lady Herbert's Garden, which was built around the remains of the old city walls. The garden was a great favourite of mine, because to my mind, it was the closest thing to being back in Donegal. Bright red and orange dahlias dominated the flowerbeds and on the old city walls, red and yellow roses climbed in and out of the crumbling stones. It was the nearest thing to the natural world in my grasp and I was eager to share it with them.

The coming of the twins may have brought its financial hardships, but it was a source of pride to my parents that we always had our school dinner money. We never suffered the humiliation of free meals. In order to achieve this, Mum would often make a game for us of scouring the house, hunting down pennies and threepenny bits in coat pockets, or down the side of the settee. Thankfully, Mum's careful budgeting meant we never went hungry, but ate lots of soup with barley, lamb stew and 'brucheen', a Donegal potato dish. Johnjoe and Charlie loved the creamy mashed potato covered with lashings of butter and salt. It was a familiar and cheap treat.

By now, as money was so scarce, the furniture had grown threadbare and the lino on the floors was curling up at the edges. There was little to show for the constant washing and polishing mum did and in frustration, she would pressgang Pat and me into helping her to rearrange the living room to make it seem a little more homely. With much pushing and pulling, the settee and the dinner table would swap places, the armchairs would be moved and the pictures on the wall would be brought down and dusted. The mantelpiece would be cleared of ornaments and replaced by some bought for a few pence at a jumble sale. Finally a bright new set of net curtains would be fixed proudly to the window to complete our makeover. It wasn't much, but it made all the difference to my mother, for it allowed her to pretend for a short time that things weren't quite so bad as they seemed. Because, however successful my mother was at controlling the family budget, Dad's heavy drinking continued to be a strain on our meagre resources. His wages as a bus conductor were low and so finances were a constant source of wrangling between both of them.

It wasn't long after we had all been reunited that I was woken from my bed by the sound of raised voices. At first I thought it was the rain bouncing off the windowpane. But then as I listened, I could hear my parents arguing downstairs. Immediately I felt anxious and rushed downstairs. They were in the living room. I stood terrified at the stairs door and watched while they shouted at each other.

"Don't speak to me like that," my father roared "Just give me a pound and I'll be out of your way."

Mum had a sour expression on her face, her mouth all twisted.

"I'm light in the head with your constant blathering. Look here's my purse. See, I've only a few shillings. It's always the same story with you, 'Give us a pound, give us a pound. You're as bad as one of the wains.'

By this point my mother was screeching at the top of her voice.

"Get out of my sight. Take the last penny I've got. And don't come back."

She threw the purse at my father.

The door slammed as he stormed out into the night. My stomach tightened; I could hear my heart pounding in my chest. Worried thoughts crowded through my brain. What would happen to us all now? Would Dad be back or was he gone for ever? By now, the whole household was stirring. My sisters, woken by the row, were crying. Mum rushed past me to pacify them. I followed her upstairs.

"What will we do now? Daddy's gone," I said.

"Don't you worry your head about that Ann," Mum spat

out fiercely. "He'll be back. You go back to bed."

It was hours later that with some relief, I heard his key turning in the lock and him stumbling upstairs, before flopping down into a drunken stupor next to Mum.

Throughout my childhood I was to hear this same row, over and over again, it was something I came to expect as part and parcel of our family life. Although I could see how much the hardships of their lives had worn my parents down, how the endless rows about Daddy's drinking had taken the romance out of their marriage, it hadn't always been this way. When my mum met my dad, he was a dashing cinema owner and had charmed her. I grew up in Coventry listening to stories of the silver screen and remembered with fondness my father's picture house in Falcarragh where I'd spent many awestruck hours as a young child in a the darkened space watching movies.

In those days, the travelling "pictures" were an important part of rural life. They provided a welcome diversion from the hardships people endured to make a living. By the fifties, the medium was becoming more popular and enterprising individuals in many small towns decided to build their own picture houses. Falcarragh was no exception and in 1957, my dad, together with his cousin John, built a small cinema on the outskirts of the town. This, he promised, was going to make our fortune.

The great advantage, when your dad owns a cinema, is that you get in free and you can see as many films as you like. So many of our evenings were spent doing just that. My mother in the box office, with Dad's cousin taking the money, smiling at the customers. My father operating the projector, and the rest of us, the audience, pressed tightly into our seats. We saw musicals, westerns and gangster films. My favourite film at the time was Mandy, the story of a deaf and dumb girl in war-torn England. Mammy and I must have seen that picture ten times. More than anything I admired her courage and tenacity, fighting against the constraints of her disability to make good. I vowed to try to be like her always.

Showing pictures was only one of my father's money-making schemes; he used to do tailoring as well and kept a shop above another cousin's hardware store in Falcarragh. My dad was a tall, pencil-thin man with a slight stoop, a long sculpted face, high cheekbones, deep-set sapphire eyes, and slicked-back, Brylcreamed hair. He moved like a dancer, graceful and even. I imagine he had stick-thin legs, because his trousers would flap about, blowing in the wind as he walked. His voice was soft and melodious and he was always throwing his head back laughing at something. An accomplished musician, he taught himself the fiddle and the piano and was not a bad singer. He would give you a song at the drop of a hat. I suppose he was handsome; he often boasted that in his younger days he'd been compared to Jimmy Stewart, the Hollywood actor. He certainly had a presence about him, an energy, an electricity. Sadly though, like many of the men in his family, he was an alcoholic and most weekends during my childhood, he spent blind drunk.

When we were in Falcarragh, I was barely aware of his drinking; I only noticed his cheery moods after he'd had a few, when he'd willingly do anything for anybody. He spent hours trying to amuse me, making paper models of giraffes and tigers, and playing tricks on me with disappearing pennies. He even let me put my finger through the gap where he had lost one of his front teeth. It seemed in those days that his good humour was boundless and his love and affection for his family unconditional.

He'd met my mum one evening when he was showing a film at Kilclooney Hall. She was in the audience and he'd taken a fancy to her right away. When she was young my mum was the epitome of an Irish colleen, with her curly auburn hair, green-flecked eyes and the sort of pale porcelain skin that models and film stars have. Over the years, I would beg my mother to tell me again and again the story of their meeting and every time she told the tale, it was different. She said he came up, sat behind her and leaned forward, putting his arm round her as he spoke.

"Hello, I'm James, James McFadden, a pal of your brother Phil here. He didn't tell me he had such a good-looking sister."

Phil had laughed.

"Take no notice of him, Nora, you want to be careful of him, he's a bevy of beauties all chasing after him."

Dad wasn't to be put off.

"What did you think of the film? Was Jimmy Stewart handsome enough for you?"

"Not really my type, I prefer Clark Gable."

He grinned cheekily back, offering her a Woodbine.

"Good crowd out tonight. Tickets sales are up. If only we could get this mob in every night, we'd be millionaires."

"Phil said you show pictures all over Donegal - is there much call for it?"

"Yes. I'm thinking of going into business with a cousin of mine, having a picture house built."

Although Mum was impressed, she wasn't going to let on. " Sounds like you've got it all worked out."

"I'm away to a dance in Dungloe next Saturday night. We'd make a handsome couple, wouldn't we? What do you say? How about a night out with a man who knows how to treat a woman."

Mum had laughed and said,

"If you think I'm going to join the posse of women chasing you, you've got another think coming. I have more sense than that."

Dad wasn't about to give up though.

"Well, you know, I never take no for an answer. Think about it and let Phil know. I'll come and pick you up."

I thought the story was very romantic and wanted to know how she fell in love with him, but she wouldn't be drawn.

Many times I would ask,

"Did you think he was handsome?"

"Now that would be telling. I married him didn't I?" Mammy would say.

By the time I was a teenager in Coventry, it seemed to me that all the romance had gone out of their lives, at least on my mum's part. In a moment of bitterness one day, she confided in me, that after six months of married life, she realised she'd made a huge mistake. It was a hard thing to hear, but I wasn't surprised, for by then it seemed she had lost all respect for him, seeing him as just another burden she had to bear.

However, after she died, I was going through her belongings when I came across a withered brown envelope. Inside was an old receipt. It was for the hotel where they had spent their wedding night. Amazingly, she'd kept it safe all through the years, through his drinking, through the rows and arguments about money. That surprised me, and made me wonder if maybe, after all, she did love him. That somewhere deep within her, the romance that they once had was still alive, the memory treasured and filed away in an old handbag.

Chapter 18 - Mammy and Me

Looking back, I realise that my mother was a mass of contradictions. On the one hand, she was strong and resilient, conquering very poor health to raise a large family, with little money and a husband who drank. On the other hand, she was incredibly vulnerable, often in a state of emotional collapse. Loving and caring, with a wicked sense of humour, she made sure there was always food on the table and we were all well cared for. She even found time to help me with my homework, which was unheard of in our house, as neither of my parents had a great education themselves.

On one occasion I sat at the kitchen table staring at my copybook, with no idea where to start. Mum stood beside me. "You've been staring at that blank page long enough, Ann. Will I help you?"

I nodded. "We've to write a story about somebody standing at a crossroads."

"Well," she said, "What about making it about someone standing at the crossroads of life and wondering which path to take?"

I'd never thought of that.

"Maybe it could be about a man deciding to join the army, or become a priest? Or a girl deciding to commit a crime?"

"That's brilliant, Mum," I said, grabbing her and giving her a big hug.

I got nine out of ten for my story and my teacher asked me to read it to the class. I was delighted.

At the other end of the spectrum, her dependence on me could be challenging. I was probably more aware of her struggles than anyone else, and, as a teenager, it often fell to me to support her and to keep her going. One night, Mum and Dad had been rowing and he'd stomped out to drown his sorrows again. The rest of my brothers and sisters had all gone to bed. We were sitting by the fire when she told me she was feeling very low. I knew that earlier in the day, she had been to the doctor's, complaining of pains in her chest and dizzy spells. She told me that, as usual, she'd been fobbed off with the advice that she should take things easy, which given her circumstances, was well-nigh impossible. She went on and on about how the doctor wasn't taking her seriously and how she was desperately worried her heart was failing.

"You know, Ann, I'm at the end of my tether. Your father couldn't give a damn; all he cares about is the drink. I can't sleep, and the pains in my chest are so bad, I could cry. Yesterday, on my way to the shops, I had to stop and steady myself by a wall. Thanks be to God I made it home. You don't know the half of it."

"Don't worry, Mum, you'll feel better after a sleep," I said, trying to find the right words to comfort her.

"But I can't sleep. I'm climbing the walls worrying about where the money's coming to pay the next bill and your father's no help. Just hands me his wages. Expects me to manage. Well I can't, not any more," she wailed.

I felt impotent; there was nothing I could do to help, I just stared at her as the tears trickled down her face. Eventually she stopped and went rooting around in her handbag. "Here you'd better take these," she said, stretching over to hand me a bottle of pills." They're sleeping tablets. I'm frightened I might swallow the lot. Put them somewhere I won't get them."

I was astounded. I'd never heard my mother talk like that before.

"Don't be daft, Mum," I managed, convinced she was exaggerating. "It can't be that bad. You wouldn't do that, Mum, you're too sensible."

Mammy shook her head. "God forgive, me but it's how I feel."

I sat looking at her as the tears streamed down her face, unwilling to believe she really meant it. Quickly I tried to marshal my thoughts. "What'll the priest say? It's a mortal sin."

"Jesus, Mary and Joseph, I know, but I can't go on like this."

"Go and see Father Thornton, that always helps. Tell him how you're feeling. It's not as bad as you think. Tomorrow you'll feel much better."

As I spoke, I knew it was a lie. Even to me, my mother's plight seemed hopeless. My father was never going to give up drinking, there was no more money to be had, and her health was probably never going to improve.

"I'll make a cup of tea. It's going to be all right. You'll see," I said as I got up and threw my arms around her, whispering, "I'll put the tablets under my pillow, and you go and see Father Thornton in the morning."

She nodded and smiled at me.

As I poured the tea in the kitchen, my hands were shaking. I could hardly hold the cup. When I returned to the living room, I found mum looking slightly calmer.

"Drink this and you'll feel better," I said, offering her the cup.

She wearily took the cup from my hand. "Where would I be without you, Ann."

Later, as I climbed into bed, I realised I'd never seen my mother this upset before. The complaints about my father were perennial: I heard them every day of my life, but something was different this time. I wondered if she was still grieving over the loss of her mother who'd died earlier in the year.

Mum had travelled over to Ireland for the funeral, but when she'd come back, she'd confided in me that at the graveside, she'd fallen on her knees, roaring and crying that she was dying. She told me that nobody knew what to do, but they carried her back to granny's and called a doctor. The doctor found nothing wrong, but she'd insisted they call a priest, who'd given her the last rites.

It seemed to me now that Mum was inconsolable, worrying she'd upset the whole family and could never look her sisters in the eye again. Now, as I lay in my bed twisting and turning, constantly checking that the pills were safely under my pillow, I recollected how I reacted when she first told me the story about the funeral. I'd tried my best to reassure her that her sisters would understand, but actually felt deeply embarrassed. Why, I'd thought, could neither of my parents behave like grown-ups?

Now, it seemed my relationship with my mother had been turned upside down and it was as if she were the child and I, the parent.

I can trace this subtle alteration in my relationship with my mother to the birth of the twins, as gradually she began treating me as a grown-up, her helpmate. I was nine years old. I felt honoured and thrilled. It didn't occur to me to resent my new role, instead I saw it as a promotion: I had been elevated to the giddy state of adulthood. I acquired a new status in the house. I lorded it over my younger brothers and sisters; my word was law, second only to Mum's. These days I would be called a young carer and if I was lucky, would possibly be in receipt of support or counselling, maybe taken on outings to the seaside, but in those days, as I was the eldest, it was expected of me.

With my new responsibilities I was often kept home from school. I don't remember minding very much, for then I was just grateful to be away from the daily grind of school and the perennial spelling tests at which I failed miserably. Looking back, I wonder if this early responsibility contributed to my later problems, even while I understand that, in asking me to help, my mother had no choice. With her ill health and young family, she couldn't have shouldered the burden alone.

One particular day stands out in my memory, possibly because of the huge thunderstorm. The sky boomed with thunder, hailstones rattled the windows and doors, and every few seconds, lightning threatened to crash into the living room, striking me dead. I was petrified. I was alone, looking after my baby sisters, while Mammy had gone into town to shop, but she hadn't returned, and the nursery, where my brothers went, was due to close for the day at any minute.

As the moments passed and still there was no sign of her, I realised, to my dismay, that the time when my brothers needed to be claimed had arrived. Putting my Wellingtons and brown gabardine coat on, I left the twins sleeping in their pram and bolted up the street. I felt afraid, but somehow brave at the same time, like Ann of Green Gables, the plucky orphaned Canadian girl I was reading about at school. More than all my fears, I desperately wanted to impress my mum, to show her how grown up I was.

At the door of the nursery, my two brothers were standing forlornly with a teacher, who was looking very annoyed. They were the only children left. They brightened up when they saw me. I gasped out an apology and swiftly lifted them into the pushchair, putting up the hood and aiming it in the direction of home. Annoyingly, the storm was showing little sign of abating and I could barely make out the road ahead. My hood was dripping water onto my face and over my eyes; my legs were raw as rain trickled down them, and they rubbed against the edge of my Wellington boots. Shards of lightening flicked through the sky, followed by loud booms of thunder. Please God, take me home safe, I prayed as I raced down the street, wildly singing nursery rhymes to my little brothers to pacify them.

As I got to the top of Cambridge street, I saw the familiar figure of Mammy struggling towards me. I was saved.

"I missed the bus, and the next one was late. Thanks be to God you were here Ann. Where would I be without you."

It was a phrase I was familiar with. Every time I heard it, I grew an inch. All at once it seemed like the sun had come out; my fears disappeared in an instant and I felt restored. All the thunder and lightning had been worth it. I had done something to please Mammy.

As I grew older, and my role expanded more and more into providing emotional support for my mother, I became quite skilled at listening and empathising. Most of mum's complaints were about my father's drinking but occasionally, things happened which were more serious and found me floundering.

I had just started secondary school when I was called into the headmistress's office. I was needed at home. As I headed for the bus, I fretted I'd find my mother at death's door. When I arrived home, my mother was sitting on her chair by the fire quietly sobbing. My heart sank. I made her a cup of tea. She could barely speak at first, but then slowly her story spilled out. A social worker had called to inspect us and finding the house untidy, with beds unmade, dishes undone and dirty cloth nappies crowding the sink, she'd threatened to take us all into care.

"Oh, Ann, what'll we do, what'll Daddy say?" Mum kept repeating over and over again, tears rolling down her cheeks.

"It'll be all right." I whispered, trying to sound reassuring. But inside, my stomach was knotted with fear. Ever since the twins had been born and the family were reunited, we'd remained under the auspices of the welfare offices, the precursor to modern social services. We had a home help, who'd only carry out the most basic of tasks, but inevitably with Mum's poor health, seven children and little money, the house wasn't always at its tidiest.

Suddenly I had a flash of inspiration. "We'll tell Auntie Mary," I gasped, "She'll know what to do."

Mum only shook her head. "We can't tell anyone. I'm too ashamed," she muttered, her face crumbling with misery.

I didn't know what to do or say. I put my arms around her. "Please don't cry, Mum, it's going to be all right." At twelve, I had little understanding of social workers and no-one to call on for support. I only knew that my mother was upset and I tried my best to comfort her.

For the next week, I couldn't concentrate at school, I kept turning the dilemma over and over in my mind, searching for a solution. The idea that we could all be shipped off into care horrified me and filled me with dread. Every evening, as I returned home on the bus from school I gazed aimlessly out of the window, hardly noticing the streets as they sped by. I felt as though I were in a trance, as if I were dreaming. Mostly, I felt powerless.

"Maybe she's forgotten," I assured Mum, when a week had passed and we'd heard nothing from the social worker. She just smiled wanly. Time went by and there was still no news. Slowly as the weeks went by and there was still nothing, my sense of anxiety began to recede into the background. My appetite returned. I felt better. As it happened, there were no further threats about shipping us into care, and in the end all that happened was that my mother's home help hours were increased. Eventually we just put it all down to experience, but even today, recalling the incident makes me break out in a sweat.

But sometimes even I failed at the responsibilities which I'd been given and I felt a huge amount of guilt. There were two paydays in our house: Friday, when Dad got his wages and Tuesday, when my mother claimed her family allowance money. The family allowance was a universal benefit paid by the government directly to the woman of the house. In those days, it was collected on Tuesday and so that day was always eagerly awaited in our house. The allowance bought much-needed spuds, eggs, bread, a bag of coal or paid the electricity bill.

One day, I realised quite how important this benefit was, when I was entrusted with the responsibility of fetching it from the post office. Mum gave me a special wallet where I was to place the few pounds and bring them safely home. That day, I remember I was in a great mood, and after I collected the notes, I ran home, singing and dancing down the street.

When I presented the wallet to my mother, she opened it and turned white. "Jesus, Mary and Joseph, what have you done. Where's the money?"

"It's in the wallet," I said.

"Well, it's not there now."

I stared in disbelief. I couldn't remember. Had I put the money in the wallet or not. I felt confused.

Mum was looking very serious and with a stern voice said, "Go back to the post office and ask them if you left it behind."

My heart skipped a beat as I set off up the street, running as fast as I could and praying the cash was still there. At the post office, the clerk assured me she had given me the money. I walked back down the street, scouring the pavement to see if the money had fallen out. There was no sign of it.

When I reached home, Mum was on the doorstep waiting for me, an anxious look on her face.

"I'll go up myself and check with the woman. You stay here and mind the wains," she said.

By now I was starting to panic. Had I really, in my carelessness, lost the family allowance? I said a quick prayer to the Baby Jesus for Mammy to find the money.

A little while later, I heard her footsteps going past the front window, her key turning in the lock. She was in tears.

"I've looked everywhere. How in the devil could you be so careless. I've no money at all, nothing at all."

"I'm sorry, I lost it. I'm sorry, Mum."

She wouldn't listen, but dragged me, screaming, into the front room and closed the door. She started to hit me as hard as she could. She was relentless. Blows were raining down on me and I was sobbing, "I'm sorry Mum, I'm sorry."

Afterwards, I lay crying on my bed, not believing what had happened. I listened to the sound of the clock slowly ticking by. An hour went by, then two. I could hear voices in the other room. I felt as if I were in a trance. But I was too ashamed to get up. I couldn't bring myself to face any of the others, let alone my mother. It felt like the worst day of my life.

In the end it was my father who rescued me. "Come on, Ann. Get up," he said gently. "Mammy's sorry: she knows you didn't mean to lose the money."

I got up and went into the living room. My brothers stared at me; my mother sat in the chair knitting, no-one said a word. Years afterwards, Johnjoe told me that my brothers had all stood outside the living room door in total shock as they heard my cries that day. They knew that my mother had never lifted a finger to me before. She never did again.

Growing up, I thought the world of my mother and would have done anything for her. I rarely argued with her, or gave her backchat, because I was worried that she was too frail, that she'd collapse and die. Even as an adult, I never fought with her or said what I truly thought. When I reflect on my life, I wonder if that early promotion to adulthood contributed to the development of my mental health problems.

Even in my sixties, I'm still confused about why I was always so desperate to please Mammy and why I never had the courage to answer her back. I often heard her say, "Thanks be to God, Ann, you never give me a pick of trouble." If I had been trouble, what then?

Later in life, I discovered that my parents had to marry when Mum found herself pregnant with me. As a child I had always been told that I was born prematurely. When I was growing up, did I sense my mother held a grudge against me for saddling her with my father and did my feelings of insecurity stem from that? Who knows. The relationship we have with our mothers is always complex and mine was no exception. To the outside world, my mother was a strong, independent woman who against all the odds — chronic ill health, poverty and a husband with a serious drink problem — saw all of her seven children safely into adulthood. To me, however, she was a fragile, troubled soul, constantly struggling to cope, lurching from one crisis to the next. I feel nothing but compassion for her, and the circumstances she found herself in. Who knows what I might have done if I were in her shoes. All I'm sure of was that she did the best she could, and for that I'll be eternally grateful.

Chapter 19 - Boom Town

In the early 1960s, Coventry was a boom town: the car industry was in its heyday and immigrants flocked from around Europe to the city. There were opportunities for everyone, with a buzz in the air and an aura of excitement and optimism that even filtered down to us children. The symbol of the Phoenix had just been added to Coventry coat of arms, to denote the post-War era of recovery and rebuilding. The city was now in full swing.

Coventry Cathedral, which had been annihilated during the bombing in 1940, but for a few remaining walls, had been rebuilt, the new building attached to the ruins of the old. Movingly, the morning after the bombing, a Cathedral stonemason had taken two charred oak beams from the debris and made them into a cross. A replica of the symbol still stands in the ruins of the old Cathedral, as a tribute to the suffering the people of the city had endured throughout the conflict.

By the time we arrived in Coventry, just twelve years after the War, the city fathers had set about a programme of rebuilding, including a pedestrianized city-centre shopping precinct, the first in Europe, and a new cathedral to stand alongside the old as a reminder of the futility of war. Coventry was growing. By the 1960s, the population was over 250,000 and there was a substantial Irish community. Men and women worked in car factories like Jaguar, Standard Triumph, Humber and also in engineering, for firms like Alfred Herbert and the electronics giant GEC. At one time, 30,000 were employed by GEC and another 100,000 in the motor industry, many of those attracted from other towns and villages around the Midlands. One journalist even claimed that the streets of Coventry were paved with gold.

Although we were Irish, and outsiders, we quickly became

part of the dream of peace and prosperity and commended every move to modernise the city. The Irish community was growing rapidly and my family was part of that. My parents were making a home for us and with each passing week, more and more friends from Donegal were arriving too. At weekends, like many other immigrant families, we came together for parties, when all our friends and family from across the city joined with us to celebrate our new life.

Our gatherings went on well into the night, the grown-ups on the chairs and the settee, with the children sitting at their feet. My mother made salmon sandwiches and apple pie, the sherry was brought out from its hiding place in the corner by the fire for the women and we would be sent to the off-licence to buy whiskey for the men. The room would be bustling with laughter as our aunts and uncles traded news from Donegal. As youngsters we listened, wide-eyed, to the conversations going this way and that.

At some point in the evening, my uncle Josie would shout, "Give us a song, James."

He wouldn't have to ask twice, for, like a shot, my father would be up, leading them in a chorus of "The Mountains of Mourne", or, "Kevin Barry". Not content with that, the audience would egg him on.

"Go on, James, go on, sing 'Paddy McIntyre's Goat'." Standing tall, glass of whiskey in his hand, a broad smile on his face, he would begin. Although we all knew the story, we still found it funny. We would be killing ourselves laughing at his expressions and actions as he sang the song about a goat who came to grief on a stick of dynamite. It was his party piece. When he'd had a few, he was a great raconteur, content to stand all night singing songs and telling stories.

When the singing was done, talk would often turn to family and friends who, like us, had left Ireland to try their luck in England. Gweedore, Gortahork and the Rosses, places I barely remembered, became the common currency of my childhood.

My favourite of Daddy's stories were those about his time as a cinema owner, in particular, "The Night of the Big Snow."

Over the years in Donegal, Dad had tried many business ventures: tailoring, running a pub and, together with his brother, showing films in church halls across the county. During the Forties and early fifties, there was hardly a parish hall in the north-west that the brothers hadn't visited, bringing Hollywood glamour to hard-pressed farming communities.

On this occasion, determined not to let their customers down, they'd bravely ventured out in a blizzard. The journey had taken twice as long as normal, with the van slipping and sliding all over the road. They eventually arrived safely and began unloading the equipment into the church hall. As usual, the place was heaving with young men and women puffing away on Woodbines, laughing and joking, waiting patiently for the show to begin.

My father was cursing and swearing, frantically searching through the reels of film he'd brought from home earlier in the evening. "I know it's here somewhere. Come on, Johnjoe, help me look for it." Johnjoe Senior was my father's brother and a partner in the business.

"For pity's sake, James, don't tell me you've forgotten it," Johnjoe said.

"Well, not exactly," Daddy admitted, although that was, in fact, the truth.

Johnjoe was about to begin the business of the evening. "Shall I collect the cash?" he asked Daddy.

"No. We can't take the ticket money until we've told them."

"Well, I'm not about to tell them. It's down to you. We'll be a laughing stock. You tell them," Johnjoe insisted.

"All right, but I'm not responsible for what they might do."

My father called for quiet and walked to the front of the

hall. "Ladies and gentlemen, can you all take a seat? By God, it's a wild night. I wasn't expecting to see so many of you."

In the front row, a young man in a bow tie quipped, "We couldn't miss a chance to see to see what them big city fellahs from Dungloe have to offer."

"Speak for yourselves," someone from the crowd added. A good-humoured laugh went up, so Dad took a deep breath. "Well, I might as well get right to it. We have a bit of a problem. Nothing too serious. Ladies and gentlemen, I'm sorry to say I have the end of the film here, but not the beginning, I must have left the other reel at home in Dungloe."

There was silence as the audience grasped my fathers' words. He went on. "Well, it's not too bad. What I can do is show the finish now and bring back the beginning next week."

For a moment no-one spoke, then one young fellah leapt up. "See the end now, wait for the beginning next week. That'd be like having the wake before the body was pronounced dead." There was a roar of laughter and everyone started to talk at once.

One woman, a regular to the events, shouted from the back of the hall. "You could go back and collect the beginning and we could wait for you."

There was a murmur of agreement.

"I'll surely be willing to do that. But with the snow, it might be a long wait. It could be hours," Daddy said.

After discussions going this way and that, it was decided to put the matter to a vote. The show of hands decided it. They would wait and send my dad back for the beginning reel, even if it took all night.

"Right, if you're sure. I'll be away then."

Tea was served and an hour passed by. There was no word of my dad. Then, suddenly he appeared at the door. A cheer went up. Raising his hand, he asked for quiet.

"Ladies and gentlemen, I'm sorry to say that the ol' van

is stuck in the snow. I need a push."

The cheers turned to dismay as they realised he hadn't even left yet. But in those days people were patient; they weren't used to having their entertainment on tap, so without further ado, a posse of eager film fans heaved and shoved him noisily off into the night. The story goes that he made it back many hours later with the missing reel, and his loyal audience settled down to watch the film as it was meant to be.

I think the reason I liked this story so much, was because it gave me a glimpse into a Daddy who was different to the man I knew, growing up in Coventry. On the one hand, I loved him deeply, but as I grew into a teenager, his angry outbursts, his treatment of my mother and his drinking tested my loyalties to the core. His outbursts were not unusual in the family: we were all used to them and took cover when needed, but one occasion sticks out in my mind solely because of how much he upset my mother. It was a Saturday afternoon and we are all watching telly. Suddenly there was a rattling in the hallway and he burst into the living room, shouting and swearing at the top of his voice.

"If I catch the divil who's had my scissors, they'll get the back of my hand. Who's been in my workroom?" He glared angrily around the room. "Own up. Who's the culprit?" he said, lunging in the direction of my younger brothers.

They all ducked out of his way.

My mother, hearing the commotion, rushed in from the kitchen.

"How the devil am I expected to finish a job if them eejits can't keep their hands to themselves," he said, before storming back inside his workroom, his lips jammed together tightly, his face purple with rage.

Mum and I followed him inside.

"Are you sure they're not here? Have you looked for them?" my mother queried, trying to calm him down.

"What do you take me for? Of course I've looked for

149

them," he roared.

"Well, it's no good shouting your head off, they must be here somewhere," Mammy said.

Dad's tailoring scissors were sacrosanct in our house: we were forbidden to touch the big heavy iron blades. Mum and I began to turn the room over, whilst he bitterly accused her of trying to sabotage him. This went on for another hour, as he angrily stood over us, bullying and shouting, whilst we searched high up and low down for the missing item. Eventually to our great relief, he stormed out to the pub, his parting words, "Those scissors better be back on my table by the time I get back, or else." I felt my whole body quiver and mum was silently weeping.

Over the next couple of hours we turned the house upside down. Eventually we found them, upstairs. No-one would own up to having moved them, but by now it didn't really matter: he'd made his point.

Afterwards I asked Mum if he had always been angry and bad-tempered. She shook her head and told me when he was younger he'd been the opposite, overflowing with wit and good humour. Through wistful tears she explained, "He changed when all the wains came along, and we hadn't two halfpennies to rub together. He was never the same again."

It was then I realised that my early memories were also of a different man, one full of warmth and tenderness. That father, I now realised, had been largely replaced by an angry, bitter individual.

Hours later he returned, blind drunk, his mood improved, the lost scissors completely forgotten.

My father had clearly changed since moving to England. Thinking about it now, he must have been facing the same sense of loss as I did, as well as the grinding poverty my mother faced every day, even if this was compounded by his spending money on drink. In Ireland, he had been a businessman: he ran a pub, he had a tailoring shop, he owned a cinema. He was also sociable, with a wide circle of friends and he loved Donegal. In Coventry, he was in a poorly paid, low-status job, with a large family to support and very few friends. And to cap it all, next to the rest of his family, he must have felt a failure: his brother was a successful businessman, one sister a radiographer, another a solicitor. It was hardly surprising he was sour much of the time.

Given all that, there were occasional times after we moved to Coventry when I caught a glimpse of the person he'd once been, a man with warmth and a sense of humour. I remember one occasion when I was very pleased to be entrusted with making my dad's tea, as Mum had a hospital appointment. For weeks ahead of the day, I planned the menu. Dad would be served up his favourite, fish in white sauce. I practised the dish several times, with mum supervising and on the day in question, rushed home from school to put the dinner on. First, I fed my brothers and sister and then when they'd had their fill, I boiled the fish gently in milk.

After five minutes, I scooped out the fish, and then carefully added the cornflour to the sauce to thicken it. Everything was going exactly to plan and I returned the fish to the sauce and left it simmering, while I set the table for Dad. Extremely pleased with myself, I drained the potatoes and glanced in at the saucepan about to serve the fish, when to my horror, I noticed that the sauce had turned a neon pink. My heart sank; I let out a yell.

Dad and my brothers came running out from the living room and we all peered into the saucepan. I couldn't believe it. Where had I gone wrong? I had faithfully followed the recipe. Tears rolled down my cheeks.

Dad tried to comfort me. "Sure the fish is fine, I'll just eat the fish, not the sauce," he offered. Tentatively I took the spatula and removed the fish from the pan and then peered into the saucepan, to find a soggy box of matches, which must have fallen off the top of the cooker into the sauce.

"Matchstick sauce," my dad brayed, laughing his socks off. He was highly amused. "Is that what you've come down to. Trying to poison me now?"

I could only gaze in horror at my aborted attempts at a sauce. I was mortified and realised I would never live this one down, but at least Daddy had managed to see the funny side of it.

Daddy could also prove himself a surprisingly competent cook, when pushed. When I was about nine, he taught me how to fry an egg. It was a Sunday morning and Mum and the rest of the family had gone to Mass. We were alone. I had been attempting to make him a fried breakfast. As I juggled the sausages, bacon and eggs, I found I couldn't get the egg yolk to white over. It sat in the frying pan, looking undercooked.

Dad leaned over, one eyebrow lifted in amusement. "Did your mother never show you how to fry an egg, Ann?"

I shook my head.

"Here let me show you."

With that, he nudged me to one side and took command. "It's easy," he explained, and lifted the edge of the frying pan, making a small well of fat on the side, which he then poured over the egg with a teaspoon. The egg turned a glossy white instantly.

He grinned and patted my head. "Now, don't tell me your daddy doesn't teach you anything."

It was only a small thing, but moments between us like that were rare and I treasured it. A few weeks later he spent several hours with me, teaching me how to press trousers. He laughed and joked as I made one unsuccessful attempt after another, trying to avoid two creases ending up on the trouser legs. At last, I mastered it, and he pressed a sixpence into my palm.

"I'll make a tailor out of you yet, Ann," he joked.

I felt my face glow with pride.

But sometimes, the old, stubborn Dad would make an

appearance. My brother Johnjoe found out he had passed five 'O' Levels, but by then had a job as an apprentice draughtsman in one of the car factories. He begged to be allowed to return to school, to do his 'A' Levels. Dad was adamant; he wasn't about to let him leave. Mum had pleaded with him, we all had, but to no avail. Eventually I cornered him in the kitchen. I pointed out the importance of seizing opportunities, and about how Johnjoe might eventually go to university.

After an hour spent arguing with him, he turned to me, his eyes misting over. "You know, Ann, I've never told a living soul, not even your mother, but I always wanted to be a doctor. I wanted to heal people. But my own father wouldn't listen, he apprenticed me to a tailor at fourteen and I never got the chance."

I was staggered. I never imagined my father had ambitions. I softened my voice, but pressed home my point anyway.

"You see. That's exactly what you're doing to Johnjoe."

He laughed. "You may as well tell him, he can quit the job."

I reached up and hugged him tight around the neck.

"Thanks, Dad, thanks for listening," I whispered in his ear.

He winked at me.

I felt elated that he'd given in, but also felt privileged by his confidences. I thought of the young man he'd been, head bent, stitching for hours, dreaming of a different life, one that never came to be, and it filled me with sadness.

When Johnjoe eventually gained a PhD., Dad was very proud, but never quite understood why he wasn't a medical doctor. He was forever complaining to him of pains in his legs, demanding a diagnosis.

At a recent family gathering I was talking to an elderly aunt, when she mentioned to me how fond Dad always was of me.

"He was always boasting about you. You were the apple of his eye."

A shiver of satisfaction shot through me and I smiled. I suppose in my heart, I knew it, but just the same, it was nice to hear. Throughout my childhood, I constantly argued with Dad. I fought with him about his drinking, about my having to do the housework, and later about politics. But at the end of it, no matter what we said to each other, I always knew he loved me. There's no doubt he was a flawed individual and a part of me can never forgive some of his shortcomings, especially his treatment of Mum. But more than anyone else, apart from my husband Charlie and my girls, he was always in my corner.

More than any of us, Dad missed Donegal. He often spoke longingly of the yellow gorse bushes that peppered the hills around our old home, sadly absent from the barren landscape of the inner city. I guess he never really committed himself to living in England and spent his life there looking back, remembering old times. Mum, on the other hand, settled well: she had wanted to leave Falcarragh and had no regrets. As well as that, Mum had two sisters living close by, who provided support and a link with home. Dad had nobody. All his family remained in Ireland and the only time he saw them was at funerals or the occasional holiday.

Not long before Dad died, my brother Johnjoe took him back on a trip to Donegal. By that time, he had suffered a series of strokes and could hardly walk. He was frail and had lost so much weight his clothes hung loosely from his gaunt and stooping frame. For most of the time he was in bad humour, constantly grumbling and swearing at my brother, who could do nothing right. One day, to pacify him, his sister Mona, who lived in Killybegs, drove him on a tour around his old haunts. When finally they approached Gweebarra Brae, they stopped, taking in the scenery. It's a lovely spot, the fierce Atlantic coming to rest in the white sands dotted like icing sugar along the edge of the sea. As they were crossing

154

over the bridge he turned his long weary face to his sister, his voice cracked with emotion and whispered, "You live in Paradise."

Our understanding of the relationship we have with our parents is often muddled, its exact nature often shrouded in the mists of time. The bond I had with my father is no exception.

Chapter 20 - The Finbarr's

If the Church was the soul of the Irish community in the fifties and sixties in Coventry, then St Finbarr's Social Club was its beating heart. Walking through the doors of "the Finbarr's" on a Saturday night was a daunting experience. The club, previously the Prince of Wales cinema, was on the busy Stoney Stanton Road, a main road leading directly into the centre of Coventry. We entered the building by climbing up a series of steep steps. Once inside, the doorman, usually a friend of the proprietor, a pint of Guinness by his side, sat resplendent in a cloud of smoke, nodding people in and out. It was wise to keep in with these guardians of the golden palace, for they acted on behalf of the owner and their word was law when it came to admissions.

Inside was a large rectangular hall with a stage at the far end, bedecked with silver and gold streamers, and twinkling lights proclaiming, "Céad Míle Fáilte" - a hundred thousand welcomes. The room would be bustling with activity, the men standing three deep at the bar under a cloud of smoke, laughing, arguing, all shouting above the din for a pint with a whiskey chaser. Covered in paste diamonds and pearls, the women sat in their satin dresses, sipping orange juices or glasses of sherry, waiting patiently for the dance to begin. Observing all this from an office high up over the front door sat the owner, huddled over his beer with his cronies, holding audiences, talking business, doing deals. He was much talked about, revered in the community. You counted yourself lucky if, on his round through the club, he acknowledged your presence with a friendly nod.

Sometime in the evening, the band would strike up to a collective moan from the men as they were dragged up to dance by their wives and sweethearts. When I was lucky enough to accompany my parents on dance nights, I sat content with a bottle of pop and packet of crisps, watching them take to the floor, my dad in his best suit, head slightly stooped, firmly squiring my mother around the room, as for once, they portrayed a picture of married bliss. Before long, the floor would be filled with couples of all ages, waltzing, doing the quickstep. Men, women and children, short and tall, thin and fat, bumping into each other, swirling and twirling round and around in time to the music.

It was at the Finbarr's that I took my first tentative steps in a waltz. As Dad led me onto the floor he said, "Now, Ann, listen to the music and follow me."

Dodging the others, he led me around the room as he counted each beat for me and I desperately tried not to step on his toes. All too soon, the tune came to an end and I was led back to my seat.

"She's a great wee dancer," he boasted to my mum, as he deposited me beside her, before reclaiming his place at the bar. I beamed with happiness and pride, knowing that in some small way, I had gained his approval.

Half-way through the evening on dance nights, the band would stop for a rest and the couples would then return to their seats for further refreshments. This was an opportunity for the newspaper vendors to begin their night's business, going from one table to the next selling The Irish Post, Ireland's Own and various regional Irish papers. These newspapers provided a precious link to home and were dutifully passed from one member of the family to the other, each piece of news gathered up and hoarded to be picked over and discussed at length over the coming week.

After the break came the traditional set dances: jigs, reels and polkas. Dancers would form into sets of four or six, dancing across to the person opposite them, with much changing and swinging of partners. Everyone in the hall seemed to know the steps and joined in enthusiastically, old and young alike, heads down, going hell for leather. Sometimes I would be dragged up to join in, hastily instructed by Mum on the various steps. A favourite at the

Finbarr's was the "Siege of Venice", or so I thought. It was years afterwards that I discovered it was, in fact, the "Siege of Ennis", a dance thought to be dedicated to a battle that took place in Co. Clare in the 17th Century.

No Saturday night was complete without the familiar rebel songs, and towards the end of the evening, volunteers from the audience were coerced into taking to the stage for a few verses of "Kevin Barry", "The Wearing of the Green", or the "Wild Colonial Boy". As the reluctant singers' voices reverberated around the hall, the appreciative audience enthusiastically joined in, first one or two, then table by table until the whole room reverberated in song.

At Christmas, the Finbarr's ran much-anticipated parties for the children of members, where we feasted on pop and crisps and selection boxes of chocolates till we made ourselves sick. Irish dancing classes were also offered and well attended by girls and boys from all across the city. One of the most popular events was bingo night, for the wives of members. My mother and my aunties met there regularly for a night of eyes-down and the all-important glass of sherry. Irish showbands performed at the Finbarr's throughout the sixties and seventies and on St Patrick's night, you could hardly get a seat.

As I grew older, I lost interest in the club, preferring to go with my friends to the Locarno, a dance hall in town. My parents, however, kept on at me to go to the Finbarr's dances in the hope that I might meet a nice Irishman there. But by the time of my late teens, I was a Coventry kid and felt out of place in this well-known bastion of Ireland. I thought it was all terribly old fashioned and certainly not the place to been seen in the Swinging Sixties.

The last time I was at the Finbarr's was on the night of my mother's funeral, when I was thirty and the youngest members of our family, my sisters, were twenty-one. Dad insisted on taking the family, for old times' sake. Earlier in the day, at Auntie Mary's, we'd had tea and sandwiches, but definitely no alcohol, which had been banned by my aunt and uncle in deference to my mother. Dad was annoyed, for he felt it was a slight on the funeral party not to offer them a drink. Even when he suggested taking the mourners to the Finbarr's, my aunt threw at him, "I don't think you should be going to the Finbarr's, James. Especially on the day of Nora's funeral. Don't you think you've seen enough of that place?"

We went anyway. At first, we sat huddled round a table, numb, too shocked to say much to each other, nursing our drinks. My dad seemed lost and alone, within himself. We were all trying our best to put a brave face on it and after a while, the familiar atmosphere of the club seeped through our grief and we reminisced about long evenings spent there in the company of our parents, with their old friends from Donegal. We talked of the lively concerts, the old-fashioned dances and the Christmas parties. We had no heart to talk of my mother. She had left us so suddenly and we felt angry, bitter. She had gone into hospital to have a heart operation, which she was assured was routine and from which she would make a good recovery. She never came round from the operation: her heart split open on the operating table. The doctor couldn't look my brothers in the eye when he broke the news to them. She was only 59.

As we left, Dad took one last look around. He whispered to my mother, as if she was still there beside him. "That's me done now, Nora. I swear to you, I'll not touch another drop."

I said nothing. I didn't believe him, but he'd never said that before. Throughout my childhood I'd always felt deeply ashamed of my fathers' drinking. At school when we talked about our parents I would clam up fearful that someone might discover my guilty secret. At no time did I ever believe he would change.

True to his word, drink never again passed his lips. To me it seemed ironic that for all their married life my parents

159

had fought over his drinking. Time and time again, my mother had begged and pleaded with him to quit. He never even tried. Now she was in her grave, he was giving it up.

In the end, sobriety came easily to him, apparently without a struggle. I never believed it was possible. If only he could have done it thirty years earlier, then maybe all our lives would have been different.

As for St Finbarr's, it gradually lost its members. Some were moved with the slum clearances into council estates on the outskirts of the city or the more fortunate into better parts of Coventry and St Finbarr's went into decline. It rattled along in the eighties and nineties, but the heart had gone out of it. The Irish community had been subsumed into the general population and somehow it had lost its *raison d'etre*. By 2007, it was up for sale, only to be burned down in an arson attack some time later. It was a sad end for a cherished symbol of Irish immigration in the fifties and sixties, when we claimed this part of Coventry as our own. When we had a little piece of Ireland in Coventry.

Chapter 21 - High Days and Holidays

During the early sixties, Coventry was a town dominated by large factories, giants in our small world, and when they called a holiday, the city rested. The last two weeks in July were known as the "Coventry Fortnight", when thousands of workers had time off and those who could afford it decamped to the coast. Skegness and Weston-super-Mare were the most popular destinations. Auntie Mary and Uncle Bill always went to Weston. We never did. For a start, Dad's jobs as a postman and then as a bus conductor didn't allow time off during the fortnight and anyway, his wages were far too low to run to a holiday. Instead, we made do with the occasional day out when we visited beauty spots around the area.

For those two weeks, the city was transformed. Gone was the constant drone of traffic on the roads and the throb of feet on the pavements. Now, everything slowed down to a more sedate, leisurely pace. It was time for poorer families to go sightseeing, to visit the new cathedral or take a trip to one of the many parks around the city. During these weeks, the town had an aristocratic feel to it, it became more refined and genteel; even the shop assistants had time for cheerful banter with their customers.

One of my favourite outings was to the Memorial Park. It was two bus rides away, so we didn't go very often and when we did, it was a special occasion. The Memorial was first opened in 1921 as a tribute to the 2,000 soldiers from Coventry who had been killed in the First World War and dotted around the park was a collection of tall trees with plaques underneath dedicated to the soldiers.

The park, which was the finest in the city, boasted an aviary, rock garden, tennis court, paddling pool and bandstand and it was all free. Whenever we went, we dressed in our best clothes, took our swimming costumes, and packed sandwiches for a picnic lunch. Whilst Mum sat on a rug having a smoke and listening to the brass band, we thrashed around in the paddling pool and then played nosy games of rounders and cricket under the trees. When it was time to head for home, rather than catch a bus, we walked down Kenilworth road and then down Warwick Road into the city centre gazing in awe at the grand houses, with their long drives, elegant gardens and high hedges. In my young days, I relished this fleeting contact with the swanky part of town, a far cry from our own tiny terrace and back yard on Cambridge Street.

Highlights of the Coventry Fortnight were undoubtedly the day trips organised by the working men's clubs to the seaside or to the pleasure parks around the Midlands. These institutions had been established over a hundred years earlier but after the War, they came into their own in Coventry.

Following the bombing of the city and the devastation it caused, working people needed new places to live in and communities to support them. So, to run alongside its housing programme, the local council allocated plots of land for the building of a few working men's clubs. These were such a success that others were established all over Coventry. Often starting out as no more than wooden huts, by the 1960s, these had been replaced by posh new buildings with concert halls and lounges.

They were non-profit-making institutions, run by committees of members. Beer was cheap, men played darts and snooker, and women played bingo. There were concerts and comedy turns for the adults and summer day trips to the seaside at Skegness, or to Whipsnade Zoo and Drayton Manor Park for the children.

There was a working men's club on the corner of the street where we lived, The Transport Club, providing recreation for the bus crews using the depot behind our house. There was another one nearby on the Stoney Stanton Road, The Stanton. Both were regularly frequented by my father, for if he was not at one, he was surely at the other. On Sundays, as dinner time came round, I would be sent to fetch him home from one of the clubs. Entering a room full of men corralled in a smoky haze, I could feel all eyes upon me as I'd find him perched on a bar stool, drunk, his nose in a pint. He would climb down, unsteady on his feet, smiling and laughing all the way home. After dinner, he would sleep it off until the evening, when he would head off again. In the winter months, whilst he slept, Mum would mischievously turn all the clocks in the house forward so that when he woke, he'd think it too late to go out. "Sure, its late now James, the pub's closed," she'd say in an apologetic tone. He'd laugh loudly, seeing through the ruse, would quickly pull on his trousers and was not to be seen again until chucking-out time.

As Dad belonged to several clubs, we got to go on two or three outings and sometimes a friend of Dad's might also donate a few tickets for others, so we were doubly blessed. It was the highlight of the summer for us, when for a day, we could pretend we were having a proper holiday, like the rest of them.

On the morning of the outing, we would progress in a line down the street, the boys first like true gents, in neatly pressed shirts with bow ties and shorts, and me and Mum in our floral prints with white gloves, pushing Mary and Carol in their pushchairs. The twins would be immaculately turned out, in straw bonnets and crisp cotton dresses, the adored babies of the family. In those days, families from across the city descended on the bus station like a swarm of honey bees, all making our way to the flotilla of buses, which had been organised for the event. Before climbing on board, we queued and were given free tickets for the rides and vouchers for lunch. Often we also got a box of goodies, containing a bottle of pop and some crisps for the journey. Before long we

163

were off, jammed in tight, mothers with children on their laps, children with children on their laps, three to a seat. We didn't care; we were just happy to be on our way. Someone would start off singing, "One man went to mow, went to mow a meadow." and before long, the whole bus would joyfully raise their voices together in song.

I remember one year in particular. Somehow my dad had wangled a ticket for Olwen to come with us. We stood together upstairs at the front of the bus, our heads sticking out of the window, for three-and-a-half hours, all the way to Skegness. By the time we arrived, we were drunk on the sweetness of the air and spent the day on the beach, making elaborate sandcastles and jumping in the waves. Later, we gorged ourselves on candyfloss and ice-cream. I had the best of times and when we arrived home, planted a kiss on my dad's shiny bald head, my gratitude for him making it possible for my friend to enjoy the day with me.

As the summers came to an end and winter drew in, I counted down the days to Christmas, to the next outings organised by the clubs, such as the pantomime. The Coventry pantomime was held at the Hippodrome, otherwise known as the Coventry Theatre, a building long gone, but in those days, it was the top venue in the town, a striking Art Deco mansion with ornate decorations, chandeliers and balconies. "The Gods", where I normally ended up watching, was higher up than I'd ever been in my life. I peered down onto the stage, squinting at the elaborate costumes and gaudy painted scenery framing the stage.

The theatre was built in the 1930s, could seat 2,000 people and had been open all through the War, despite the bombing. It was renowned for its pantomimes, which took a full year in their planning, in the scenery workshop in the old Plaza cinema and in the wardrobe department in a disused garage in Quinton Road. Its heyday was in the fifties and sixties, where it drew big audiences to its variety performances, featuring everyone from The Beatles to the Royal Ballet.

For what seemed like hours, I queued with my brothers and sisters and hundreds of other children waiting for the doors to open. We were a needy bunch: our parents were hard-up and for some families, the pantomime was the high point of Christmas. Now, we grabbed the excitement and wonder of the day with both hands.

The pantomime would be my first experience of the theatre, and it was delicious, like chewing all my favourite sweets at once, every single bit a delight. I saw *Cinderella, Jack and the Beanstalk, Sleeping Beauty* and *Aladdin,* all courtesy of the working men's clubs. The pantomime transported me to a make-believe world, full of beautiful ladies, glitzy costumes, handsome princes and diabolical villains. I screamed, "He's behind you", and, "Oh, no it isn't," till I was hoarse, making myself sick on the contents of the selection boxes supplied by the clubs. It awakened my imagination to the magic of drama, it spiced up my playtime with a myriad of colourful characters and it enriched my education.

Sadly, the days of the working men's clubs have largely passed, having given way to pubs and city-centre nightclubs. The ones that are left limp by, with dwindling customers and soaring costs. The large factory employers disappeared in the seventies and eighties and with them, the works-based communities that these clubs served. The working classes still exist in the city, but they are more disparate now, scattered about in a myriad of occupations. Also, communities have changed and with them, the way people spend their leisure time. The clubs can't compete with the cheap booze offered by the supermarkets, and families don't go in vast numbers to weekend variety concerts. It would seem that the basis for the existence of working men's clubs has vanished and with them that symbol of working-class Britain that they represented. I, for one, mourn their passing.

Chapter 22 - Revisiting the Old Country

Growing up in the heart of the city I often dreamt longingly of the meandering country lanes and dappled hills I had left behind me in Donegal. But by the time we went back there on holiday, my family were well settled in Coventry and although I still considered myself Irish, for all the world I looked and sounded like an English girl. I was happy in my identity as a city girl, and although Ireland was my homeland, that first time we returned, I found I no longer had that sense of belonging I once had. On holiday we boarded on Granny's farm, where life, I found, resembled something from the set of *The Quiet Man*, the popular film starring John Wayne and Maureen O'Hara: it was somehow unreal, old fashioned, a far cry from the Ireland I remembered in Falcarragh.

Granny lived in a thatched cottage in Loughfad, a very rural part of south Donegal and, from that base, we visited friends and relatives around the county. These days, there are no more than a dozen permanent inhabitants in Loughfad, but in the sixties, it probably contained a hundred people, subsistence farmers with extended families owning a herd of cattle, a pig, maybe some chickens. Everyone in the townland was related in some way, all working the land, supporting each other, through the good and lean times.

My grandparents' whitewashed cottage had been built in the 1840s by my great-grandfather, whose family had farmed the land there for several generations. At the front of the cottage, lupins grew in profusion along the cracks in the walls and the scent of phlox and roses in the garden floated in through the half-door. Beyond was the orchard, groaning with apples, alongside gooseberries, blackcurrant and raspberry bushes. It was roomy inside, with a kitchen and two large double bedrooms. The kitchen was bright and busy, with numerous holy pictures decorating the walls. At one side, by a window overlooking the garden, stood a scrubbed pine table and chairs, and on the other wall, facing it, was a well-worn leather settee. On the back wall sat a big wooden dresser decked with brightly coloured blue crockery. Beside this was a small scullery, where the water from the well and the milk churn were kept, behind a curtain. The flagstones on the floor were brightly polished and covered with well-worn rugs. The open fire of the past had been replaced by a black range, a cast-iron stove that provided heat, a surface to cook on, and an oven for the copious scones of bread which were always on the go. When we visited, there was still no running water or electricity in the cottage, and outside they had a foul-smelling hut where you went to the toilet. Although it was the mid-sixties, the rural electrification scheme that modernised post-War Ireland had yet to reach Donegal. At night, lamps flickered in the glow of the evening, providing dim light as we all sat round talking and listening to the battery-operated radio.

Family life, for my mother, had been one of hard work from an early age. As a girl, she and her sisters knitted and wove tweed, a Donegal tradition, night after night, for a few shillings to buy clothes, shoes and sugar. The rest of what they needed, they produced themselves. The children helped with the chores on the farm before school and they grew potatoes, cabbages, turnips, carrots and wheat, which they took to the mill to be ground into corn to make bread. Every year, a pig was reared, which was slaughtered for bacon. They also kept hens and ducks, so the family had a plentiful supply of eggs and what they didn't eat, they sold on to the local shop.

Returning to Ireland on holiday, I felt delighted to be spending time in my mother's childhood home soaking up the atmosphere of rural Ireland once again.

My mum and her six brothers and sisters were born in the cottage. However, by the early sixties, only my granny and Auntie Brid remained in the house. Although I was only six when my grandfather passed away, I remember him as a giant of a man, well over six feet tall, with a shock of white hair and a walking stick. He was quiet and gentle, his voice soft and melodious, his conversation slow and deliberate. He loved dogs and always had a black and white collie by his side. He seemed to have endless patience and was full of stories of the leprechauns and the banshees who clung round the hedgerows, whistling in the wind.

As I child, I was told he had travelled to America in his twenties, and I have often wondered what conditions must have been like for him, going all that way at the turn of the century. Whilst on a trip to New York, for my fiftieth birthday, I discovered his name amongst the records of the millions who had landed on Ellis Island, seeking a better life in America. I found out that he had set sail from Derry, in 1903, on a ship called the SS Columbia. When he arrived, he must have been bewildered as he stood in line, his eyes, his face, his feet, his heart, his neck, his lungs and his scalp all closely examined for defects and evidence of disease.

When I visited the museum on the island, the photographs of the would-be immigrants showed a pitiful bunch of half-starved, terrified individuals tamely submitting themselves to poking and prodding by ranks of anonymous men in uniform. He was one of the lucky ones, he was fit and healthy, so when his cousin Francis McCloon turned up to collect him a few days later, he was allowed to leave and to settle in Brooklyn.

I know very little of his life in America, apart from the fact that he worked in the gold mines of San Francisco and survived the great earthquake there in 1906. I got the impression, growing up, that he loved America and I was always curious as to why he'd returned. I recall, not long before he died, asking him if he had been sad to come home. He had looked down at me with his soft brown eyes and winked. "Never for a minute, for then I met your granny and fell in love."

From what I recall of Granny, she had steely eyes that bore right through you, scraped-back hair and was always dressed in a black skirt, a blouse with a high collar and wore a brightly coloured brooch at her throat. She was a stickler for cleanliness and she ran the house with fairness and efficiency. To us, she made it very plain she didn't approve of my father, so whilst we stayed there on our holidays, he went off to be with his family in Dungloe. Granny had a sharp tongue; she ordered everyone about and could be demanding and impossible to please. But she had another side to her. She loved to tell stories and when she did, her face would light up with warmth and humour.

On that first trip home she gathered me and my brothers round the kitchen table and began her story. "I called into the duck house one day and found the damn fox had killed all my ducks. Thanks be to God, he'd left the eggs untouched. They were still warm, so I slipped them under a brown speckled hen. She was a good wee bird and sat on, till one day the ducklings hatched out. The hen took to them right away: she mothered them and led them round the yard, proud as punch. One day I said to myself, wouldn't it be grand if I learned those ducklings to swim? I fetched a big bowl from the kitchen, filled it with water and laid it on the ground. I called the ducklings over and as soon as they saw the water, they jumped in, and started swimming. I couldn't believe it, and the hen couldn't either: she raced round demented, clucking, and calling her brood. They took no notice and carried on swimming, smart as you like."

I was mesmerised by her story and was desperate to meet the hen and her ducklings. She sighed. "That was a good few years ago; the hen's long gone. Now, don't tell anyone, for I'm sure they'd think your granny was light in the head to be at such nonsense."

"I don't think you were light in the head, Granny. You were so clever, teaching the ducklings to swim."

She smiled and patted me gently on the head. "You

might be a city girl now, but you still understand Donegal ways."

My father's father, CP, kept a chicken farm on a tennis court at the back of his bungalow in Dungloe. In his younger days, he had built up a successful electrical business, selling and repairing TVs and radios, and had only taken to poultry later in life. He was a tall, bony man, who suffered from a condition of the spine that left him stooped over. Always immaculately turned out in a starched collar with a tie, his shoes shining, he could be charming, especially to his customers or when he'd had a drop or two. By the time we came on holiday he lived alone, his wife having died shortly after I was born. My mother once confided in me that throughout their married life, he'd led my grandmother a merry dance, but was inconsolable at her passing, blaming himself for sending her to an early grave.

As a child I found him scary, for in the privacy of his home, he had a fierce temper, and was given to cursing loudly at the slightest transgression. He was especially dismissive of anything my father said and would often compare him unfavourably to my uncle Johnjoe, his other son, whom he adored. But he had a soft spot for my mother. When we arrived to stay, he would wander off to the back of the house, catch a squawking chicken by its neck and, as my brothers and I stared, open-mouthed, would swing it around his head, until its lifeless body trailed like a fag-end from the palm of his hand. Smiling broadly, he would present his offering to my mother, dressed in her best holiday clothes, to pluck and gut for our tea. His generosity didn't end there. Every Christmas he parcelled up a dead bird and sent it through the post to us in Coventry. It would arrive, sometime after Christmas Day, wrapped in brown greaseproof paper and string and stinking horribly. I don't know what the postman thought of our gift, for by the time he delivered it, was only good for the dustbin.

After my maternal grandfather died, Granny and Auntie Brid couldn't manage the farm so by the early sixties, it was taken over by my uncle Tommy, who lived with his family in a cottage opposite. From our base at Granny's, me and Pat and Johnjoe teamed up with Tommy's children, Kathleen, Michael and Tommy, and amused ourselves roaming the fields and hills around the cottage, foraging for nuts in the hazel woods nearby, and gorging ourselves on gooseberries from Granny's orchard.

To me it was a magical time, spent running free, with no curfews or neighbours to shout at me for trespassing. Best of all, when the weather improved, I was allowed to help with gathering in the hay.

Working in the fields, like Mum had done when she was a girl, was a great novelty. She had no choice about it and I often heard her complain about the long hard days, adults and children alike with no shoes on their feet, toiling from dawn till dusk. By the time I came on holiday, this was still a reality for my cousins, who each had their jobs to do around the farm. They never complained, but seemed delighted to introduce their city relatives to this annual ritual. I was enthralled and joined in enthusiastically, for it was all part of the thrill of my holiday. Rising early in the morning, my brothers and I joined our uncle and his family in the field, where the hay lay drying in the sun. With a wooden rake, I worked all day without a break, gathering the hay into small tramcocks, which rose up over the field like termites' nests. My fingers would be blistered, my legs bitten raw by insects; I would have a headache from the afternoon sun, but I didn't care. It was the best entertainment. The day was filled with laughter and fun, and screams of pleasure and delight when we spotted tiny field mice scampering amongst the hay. The labours would end with a cool drink of buttermilk, languishing on chairs outside the front of the house whilst we proudly surveyed our work.

Later, whilst the adults were getting the tea ready, I would be allowed to churn the milk and make butter. Round and round with the paddle I would go, clunk, clunk, clunk, in the narrow wooden pail, my arms aching, until it was finished. Then, I'd watch in admiration as Auntie Brid gathered up the butter and patted it into squares, all ready to eat. If I was lucky, I would be given buttermilk from the churn.

Whilst at Granny's, I feasted on a diet of homemade bread, fresh eggs, fresh milk and butter, which I loved. The downside was that before long, I would be covered from head to toe in itchy hives, a reaction to all the fresh produce and would have to endure a treatment of baking soda about my body for the rest of the holidays.

As there was no running water in the cottage, we children were often tasked with the job of fetching it from the well at the front of the house. It was a great novelty to lower the bucket into the clear sparkling water and carry it safely inside to be used to boil vegetables for our Sunday lunch.

Sundays in Loughfad were special and had a certain magic all of their own. The morning would begin with a simple breakfast of boiled eggs, homemade bread and jam. Then Mum would bundle us into our Sunday best, ready for the long walk to Mass. While all this was going on, my Auntie Brid would be running up and down to her room, trying on clothes, deciding what to wear, changing from one outfit to another. She was particularly fond of hats and had dozens of hat boxes piled high over her bed. The hats were of every shape and size, some of soft felt, made to be pulled down over the face, others, small stiff caps decorated with coloured netting, coyly covering the eyes. She had never married but was always "doing a line" with someone. A handsome woman, she smelled of lavender water and face powder and always dressed immaculately, in dark skirts and silk blouses and high-heeled shoes.

She might have been a fashion plate, but after a hard day's work she had a habit of planting herself squarely in front of the hearth, lifting her skirt and warming her backside by the fire. As children we sniggered to each other as we caught a glimpse of her long, pink flannelette drawers. She worked as a supervisor in a knitwear factory in Glenties and cultivated a rather posh accent. I was in awe of her. She was kind enough, but viewed me and my brothers and sisters as something of a minor irritation.

When we were all ready, prayer books and rosaries in hand, white gloves and hats in place, we set off, the adults following by car. The boys and girls went first, walking the mile or so to church, led by our cousins, who cheerfully pointed out relatives' cottages and favourite spots by the lake where fish could be easily caught. We skipped along the road, delighted to be out in the countryside, far away from all the bustle of our city roads.

Mass at Kilclooney chapel was made entertaining because one side of the church was always racing against the other in their responses to the priest. It ended up as a rather musical jumble of Latin phrases – the Mass in English had yet to arrive in Donegal – echoing back and forth, through the chapel. When it was done, we all piled into the shop next door for Sunday papers and a penny's worth of sweets, to sustain us on the long walk home.

On one level, I envied the life my cousins had: their closeness to nature, the free and easy atmosphere of the countryside, but on another, was glad when it was time to return to Coventry. Ireland might have been the place I was born and where I spent my formative years, but by the time we came to holiday there, it didn't feel like home any more. By then, I had more in common with my friends back in Coventry. We wore the same clothes, followed the same football team and watched the same programmes on TV. I was just discovering the pop scene and had started going to

173

discos. By contrast, my cousins followed showbands and went to country dances, something I turned my nose up at. It also seemed to me I had more choices about my future: I wouldn't be tied to a farm, or working on the land, but might end up with an interesting job in industry or in the civil service. My brothers, also, would have more opportunities: they could be apprenticed to one of the car factories, learning a trade. It was different for my parents, their ties were much deeper, they had grown up there, been adults in Donegal. They belonged.

Over those years spent on holiday, I had grown very fond of my cousins, but as the sixties drew to a close, I felt I was poles apart from them. We led very diverse lives, they in the country, me in the city. We even spoke differently. I enjoyed coming on holiday, dipping into their lives, but had no desire to make them my own. The idea of bringing the cows in every night and sitting milking them each morning filled me with horror. The farmyard might have been entertaining in small doses, but it was also smelly and according to my cousins, the work was never ending.

The last holiday we had all together at Granny's was when I was about sixteen and as we all stood on the doorstep saying our goodbyes, I felt sad to be leaving, but realised I felt like a stranger. My stay in Donegal had been enjoyable and I would always treasure the memories it created, but I didn't feel part of that world any longer. By now I'd slipped on a smart new identity, cloaking my Irishness far beneath. It felt liberating. Our house in Hillfields might have been miles from any green space, nowhere near the sea, but it felt right to be returning to the damp, overcrowded end-terrace where I now felt I belonged.

Chapter 23 - Loving Creations

Even though we were now well and truly Coventry kids, there were still so many reminders of our Irishness at home, not least of which were the hand-knitted sweaters that Mum regularly made. When we were all youngsters, we loved them so much we would compete over whose would be made first. "Make mine next," Johnjoe would plead.

"No, me, it's my turn," Pat would insist as he would elbow Johnjoe out of the way and boldly stand in front of Mum as she sat with the hanks of wool dangling in her lap.

She would be in no mood for disagreements and would wag her finger warningly. "Not another word. I've plenty of yarn for both of you, so you needn't argue. Here, Pat, fetch me the tape and turn round so I can measure you up."

This argument was a regular feature in the house. With seven of us to clothe and feed, Mum was forever trying to save a bit of money by knitting our jumpers and cardigans herself, but we always competed fiercely for who would be first to wear her latest creation.

The production of the hand-knits was a family affair. Firstly, Mum would visit Coventry Market to buy the yarn, the market's vast circular dome housing stalls selling fruit and vegetables, clothes and general goods of every description. There, amongst the flurry of busy shoppers, she would spend what seemed like hours sifting through the different quality wools. There were thick, rope-like yarns, which could be knitted up quickly, or soft feather-like ones, invariably too expensive and beyond our reach, and my mother's favourite: coarse, strong, fibrous wool she knew would be hard-wearing and not shrink. When the choice was finally made, there would be the inevitable haggling over the price. How much if we bought one colour in bulk? Could they offer a discount? At this point, I was usually cringing with embarrassment.

Back home, hanks were held aloft on my eager young

arms, as Mum unwound the wool into tight balls, ready for knitting. When her jobs were done for the day, she would sit in her seat in the corner and knit, the needles click-clacking like tap dancers' feet, creating the most complex of designs whilst glued to the television set. Such was her skill, she hardly ever made a mistake or dropped a stitch. Somehow, she invented all her own designs, which she fashioned into all manner of garments, never using a pattern. Once they were finished, we were happy to be proudly paraded down to Sunday Mass. I would be in a knitted suit of pink or green, my favourite colours at the time. Pat, Johnjoe, Charlie and Mick would sport matching flecked sweaters and Mary and Carol would be much admired in their intricately patterned woollen dresses.

Putting clothes on our backs was the least of the worries in our house. As well as Mum's great knitting, we had the benefit of Dad being a tailor, both true Donegal skills. Before we left Ireland, he had a shop in Falcarragh, but in Coventry, he only worked at it in his spare time. Throughout my childhood, there was a sign on the front window of our house advertising the making of fine suits and alterations.

Dad worked his magic in the downstairs bedroom, which doubled as his workshop, where he kept his sewing machine, bolts of cloth, his cutting table, his pattern books and all the other accoutrements connected with tailoring. The room smelled of stale smoke and tweed, a heavy, languid masculine smell which I always associated with him.

"Dad. There's somebody here for alterations," I would screech from the front door.

Moments later there would be a clattering from within and he would emerge, fag hanging from his lips, to invite them into his den with a bad-tempered growl, where a job would be commissioned. Most commonly, it was for trousers to be shortened, waistbands expanded, or elbows of jackets patched. Occasionally a suit might be ordered. This was the desirable job, for he could turn a good profit on one. If he did get an order for a suit, he would present his client with an array of thick pattern books, from which a choice of cloth could be made. Then he would set about the business of ordering the material, drawing and cutting out the design, tacking it together with long black stitches and, finally, sewing it up on his machine. Then there was the inevitable fitting, when he would hold his breath that no mistakes had been made. After this, we would hear him banging away with his heavy iron, pressing the garment into shape.

Over the years, he made dozens of suits and I never once heard of an unappreciative paying customer. However, my brothers were quite a different matter. At some stage, my parents decided that Dad would make suits for all my brothers – on reflection, it was probably for a family wedding, or a visit to Ireland. The problem was, he only had one pattern, dating from his heyday in the Forties. Whilst his customers, invariably older men like himself, appreciated an old-fashioned, well-cut garment, my brothers, especially the older ones, longed for something modern and fashionable. My dad didn't do fashionable.

In no time at all, my father had conjured up four new suits. Although the two youngest boys were quite content with their new outfits, Pat and Johnjoe objected strongly, saying that they would be ridiculed by their friends for wearing such outdated clothes. It was the time of jackets with wide lapels and flared, bell-bottomed trousers and my dad had produced jackets with slim lapels and straight drainpipe trousers. They complained loudly to Mum, and to anyone else in the family who would listen. Dad was adamant. He had laboured over them and like it or lump it, they would be worn. And so it was, identical in colour, pattern and style to each other, they were worn by my brothers till the backside on the trousers grew shiny and the jackets got too small, when, to my brothers' relief, they could be eventually be abandoned to the rag-and-bone man.

Pat suffered in other ways, too. Times were hard and as a way of saving money, Dad hit on the idea of shortening his old busman's trousers to fit Pat for school. Although the legs fitted, they were far too long in the body and Pat had to wear braces under a sweater to hold them up. Once, to his great embarrassment, he had to take his jumper off and the whole class laughed to see the state of his trousers.

By the late 1960s, my tastes in clothes and those of my oldest brothers, had grown more sophisticated and both Mum's and Dad's efforts to clothe us were scoffed at. Growing up, I had considered myself fortunate to be seen in Mum's knitted creations but, in my teenage years, I longed for shop-bought clothes, dainty cardigans and jumpers, not the chunky hand-knits Mum produced.

Later, when I was nineteen and about to get married, I was shocked to hear my friend, who had agreed to make my bridesmaids' dresses for nothing, appeal to Mum to knit her an Aran sweater in return. The Aran patterns were traditional and passed down from family to family in the west coast of Ireland. It was said if there was a drowning at sea, a body could be recognised by the pattern of his sweater. Mum's pattern had been passed down through the family. I couldn't believe anyone would want to wear one of those old-fashioned cardigans Mum still insisted on turning out. In the end she made two, one for my friend and one for her husband. They were both thrilled.

These days, I am in awe of the labour this must have taken, the skill, the workmanship. We were fortunate in that both our parents were gifted craftsmen. Whilst for the most part, I appreciated Mum's efforts, I always overlooked Dad's. I never gave a thought to the hours of hard graft he put in over and above his day job, doing alterations and making suits, trying to earn a bit of extra cash to keep the family afloat. Often, I watched him after a long day at work, tired, head down, cranky, labouring away on his sewing machine, night after night and never took the time to say, "thanks for all your hard work." I wish that I had.

Chapter 24 - St Patrick's Day

One opportunity to commemorate our Donegal roots and our Irish heritage was presented by St Patrick's Day. As a family, we were happy to announce to the world we were Irish and never passed on an opportunity to celebrate. For weeks ahead, I looked forward to the day with relish, when my parents would meet up with family and old friends to enjoy themselves, a day which would end with the inevitable St Patrick's Day dance at the Finbarr's. The St Patrick's Day Dance was the most important social event in our calendar and everyone in the community was there, from the dustman to the parish priest.

For weeks before the big day, my pennies would be hoarded and then Olwen and I would head off to the delightfully named Catholic Repository at the top of our street to choose my St Patrick's Day badge. We'd push the door open nervously, a bell would ring and the proprietor would emerge from her back room.

Mrs Thompson was a tiny roly-poly of a woman, all smiles and instantly at our command. It didn't matter if we had a penny or a pound to spend, we were always treated like millionaires. The shop, which was bright and light, with the sun streaming in from the large shop front, smelled of polish and new books. Walls were hung with holy pictures and the shelves stacked high with prayer books, boxes of Miraculous Medals, rosaries and statues of the Virgin Mary.

The badges were always kept in a brown cardboard box under the counter and at my command, the lid would be lifted and the treasures from within, wrapped in tissue paper, would spill out onto the counter. Badges were shaped like Irish harps, St Patrick's staff or shamrocks and decorated with green ribbon, wafer-thin gold paper and tiny sparkling gems. I thought that they were wonderful, fragile concoctions, too good for the likes of me.

Choosing a badge was a serious business and day after day, I would revisit the shop, studying the selection, carefully turning them over in my hand, and alternatively holding them up to the light and against my chest, until I settled on one. Cost was always a consideration and, bless her heart, Mrs Thompson would smile knowingly, wink and knock a few pennies off, when I was wavering between one I really wanted and one I could afford.

In those days, a St Patrick's Day badge was an essential item for an Irish child and something to be marvelled at, however now, it's a custom long gone and although a small number are still made, you rarely see one, even in Ireland. But when I was a small child, I couldn't wait to get to school to show my friends, to compare mine with theirs and to see whose was best.

At St Mary's, St Patrick's Day began with the singing of "Hail Glorious St Patrick" at the tops of our voices, followed by a talk by the headmaster on the story of the great saint. Sitting cross-legged in the assembly room, we were spellbound as we listened to how St Patrick banished the snakes from Ireland and converted the Irish to Christianity. I imagined him standing, Christ-like, on a hill, preaching to a vast crowd of people, with the Holy Spirit, sheathed in a billowing white cloud behind him, his wise words mesmerising the crowds.

When assembly broke up, we'd file out and then try to catch a glimpse of each other's badges and fight about whose was best. Predictably, the children with the more affluent parents had the most colourful and stylish badges, and children whose parents couldn't afford badges, just wore shamrocks. All the adults wore shamrocks imported from friends and relatives back home. My parents' shamrocks had been carefully gathered from the fields around Granny's in Donegal and lovingly pressed into small, square green boxes and posted across the water to us, to arrive rather limp and in need of good soaking, before being pinned proudly to

Mammy and Daddy's chests.

In Falcarragh, the highlight of my St Patrick's Day had always been the town parade, when no expense was spared to put on a good show. Before my family left Ireland, I had stood in awe as John Kelly, a good friend of my dad's, led the procession, throwing his mace high up in the air, twirling and whirling it round, till the onlookers grew dizzy watching him. The street was filled with the high-pitched notes of the tin whistles, the beat of drums and the thud of dancing feet as classmates and friends alike, dressed in all shades of green, thrilled and impressed me with their skill. I was spellbound, and felt so proud to know John.

The 17th of March wasn't a bank holiday in England, so the St Patrick's Day parade in Coventry had to be held at the weekend when, it seemed to me, the atmosphere and sense of excitement of the actual day had passed. Even though marching bands and Irish dancers were bussed in from across the city, from the West Midlands and further afield, I felt adrift from it all. It didn't seem like the kind of parade I was used to. It was too remote and impersonal. Instead, I longed more than anything to be back on the main street in Falcarragh, standing on the pavement, waving my Tricolour and cheering as my friends and neighbours processed up the street.

The parade might have been a disappointment, but my parents still made the most of St Patrick's Day by attending the dance at the Finbarr's. Every year it was the same routine. Mum would visit the hairdressers in the afternoon and then spend all evening getting ready. Dad always had the day off work and spent most of it at the pub. Eventually at about seven o'clock, he would appear at the front door, and arm-in-arm, my parents would stroll up the street smiling and chatting about old friends from Donegal whom they hoped to meet at the dance.

Over those years, Mum wore a powder-blue chiffon

dress she kept for special occasions and a crystal necklace Pat and I had bought for her birthday. I can see her now, pretty as a picture and smiling broadly.

My job for the night was to babysit. I didn't mind, because my parents left money for sweets and we enjoyed our own celebrations, with bottles of pop, crisps and Milky Ways. One year in particular stands out, when my father's cousin, from Birmingham, surprised us by turning up at the front door with chocolates and whiskey for Mum and Dad, dolls for me and my sisters and toy cars for my brothers. Mum conjured up a salmon salad, followed by lashings of tea and homemade apple pie. I stood, open-mouthed, listening to the excited chatter as they swapped news from Donegal before all disappearing up the road that evening to the Finbarr's.

Sadly, as the years went by, St Patrick's Day came to mean less and less, to me and my brothers and sisters, till in the end it was only my parents who celebrated it. By the time I was at secondary school, the allure of the St Patrick's Day badge had begun to wear off and the memories of the celebrations in Donegal were receding. Secondary school was leading the way into a bigger world, where mods and rockers, the Beatles and the Swinging Sixties beckoned loudly. I was leaving my Irish roots behind.

I was becoming English.

I'm certain that by the time I was eleven my accent was indistinguishable from those of the hundreds of other Coventry girls and boys who attended my school. Cardinal Wiseman's was huge and included a girls' grammar school, a girls' secondary modern and a boys' secondary modern. It was Catholic and children came from across the city, travelling on a specially commissioned fleet of buses, which left us on the doorstep each morning. The pupils were mainly born and bred in Coventry but most had parents who were from other parts of the United Kingdom, Ireland, Poland and the Ukraine. Only a small minority were originally from

Coventry. We were a mix of backgrounds and traditions, our mothers and fathers economic migrants to the city in the late fifties and early sixties.

Of all the newcomers, I felt closest to the girls from the Polish community, whose families had been in Coventry since the War. Most had fled from occupied Poland or came to join the Polish Air Force, which was operating in Bramcote, near Coventry, during the War. The Polish community was one rich in tradition and culture, with its own churches, shops and clubs.

Like the Irish, Polish immigrants had strong links to the Catholic Church and hence, lots of their children were educated in Catholic schools. All the girls had strange, long names which I found difficult to pronounce. My impression was that they tried hard at everything and were invariably top of the class. They were nice, friendly, unpretentious pupils and like me, they were also trying desperately to fit in.

Along with most of my friends, I didn't pass my eleven-plus and ended up in the "B" stream in the secondary modern school.

Prior to 1967, Britain had a two-tier education system, with those judged the brightest entering grammar school and the rest, the secondary modern. The passport to grammar school, to academic study and assumed long-term affluence was the eleven-plus exam. Only Johnjoe in our house made it over this hurdle. All the rest of us were educated at Cardinal Wiseman secondary modern I had no expectations of passing the exam: too often my school reports were awash with Cs and Ds and comments like, "doesn't concentrate."

In those days, Cardinal Wiseman's was run by Irish nuns, with help from a team of lay teachers, many of whom were also Irish. However, at school we learned nothing of Ireland. My two favourite subjects, history and literature, were all about England. I fell in love with the novels of Jane Austen and the Brontës. The Regency balls and the wild

184

Yorkshire moors took my fancy. I imagined myself taking tea with Elizabeth Bennet and dancing at a ball with Darcy, revelling in the wit and the romance of it all, then tramping through the moorland with the wind whistling round my ears, as Heathcliff calls desperately for Cathy. I also developed a love of English history, a passion that stays with me still.

As I explored the pages of my school books, taking in the splendour of the Tudor courts, the triumph of the Armada, the great British inventions of the 19th Century, I felt proud. I wasn't English, but somehow, I became part of it: it felt like my history. Britain's empire may have been falling apart by this time, but the teaching in school still engendered a sense that to be British was something special. Something to be aspired to.

At home, too, the talk was no longer of de Valera, or the Free State, but of the Labour Prime Minister, Harold Wilson, and his "white hot technological revolution" My father was a Labour Party supporter, we read the Daily Mirror and we began to see ourselves as no different from the other working-class families in Coventry. We had the same values and aspirations. Gradually, my Irish identity was being eroded and replaced by a new one that fitted more closely to the world around me.

My brothers played football at school and supported the Sky Blues, the local Coventry team. They could never afford to go to the matches, but watched with baited breath on TV as their team fought its way up from the third to the first division over the course of the 1960s. When Coventry were promoted from the third division, I remember all the kids in the playground marching in a long line shouting, "Up the Sky Blues." To cap it all, England got to the final of the World Cup in 1966 and our whole family gathered around the TV to watch. Even though we were an Irish family, we were rooting for our adopted country.

As I left my childhood behind and went into my teens, a new

world was opening up around me. I was starting to take an interest in boys, but refused to go to dances at St Finbarr's, which now seemed old fashioned and played outdated music. Instead, I headed to the Locarno Ballroom in the city centre, along with my friends and danced to the Beatles and the Rolling Stones, catching the last bus home at eleven o'clock. It was there I discovered port and lemon, and met my first boyfriend underneath the flashing lights of the disco. By the time I was seventeen, the transition from Irish child to English teenager had been accomplished without much trauma.

It was cool to be English in the sixties. On a trip home to Donegal when I was about sixteen, I became reacquainted with a cousin my age. We hung out together, went hitchhiking, visited family. She admired my daring miniskirts, my hair, my style, everything about me, but especially my Englishness. She asked about the Beatles, the dances, the English boys. I was flattered and delighted with my new identity.

I've often wondered what makes us feel at home in one identity rather than another. Is our identity a reflection of our roots. Do we learn it from our culture, or is it something less tangible. A friend from Northern Ireland maintained that it was only by a whisker that Donegal had been retained by the south in 1921, instead of becoming part of Northern Ireland, as I reflected on this I decided I was proud of my Irish heritage no matter which side of the border I ended up on.

When I first emigrated from Ireland in 1959, I missed Donegal hugely, but gradually came to love England, my adopted country. But when I was growing up in Falcarragh, I had come to believe that being Irish was something to be valued and cherished. That belief had never left me.

During the Troubles and the IRA bombing campaigns that took place in the seventies and eighties, it was an advantage not to be identified as Irish. By then, everyone assumed I was

English, so I did not have to endure some of the abuse that came the way of the Irish. My parents were very fearful, especially following the Birmingham bombings. They kept their heads down. They worried that they might be targeted, or suffer humiliation or ridicule. I have heard from many sources of Irish people facing unpleasantness and prejudice back then.

My Uncle Bill was a surprising target. He was born in Yorkshire but had an Irish surname, as his father was Irish. Colleagues at work constantly taunted him to go back to where he was from. It was a very trying time for him and his wife. He kept quiet and eventually it stopped: they found another target for their frustration . The prejudice in Ireland was just as bad, albeit in the other direction. During the Troubles, my brothers visited Donegal and found themselves the brunt of anti-English sentiment, when they were referred to disparagingly as "Brits", and told to go home.

The complex interaction involved in belonging to two countries yet fully to neither, must have impacted upon many people at the time. The tens of thousands of Irish who'd made their way to England settled and raised "mixed families" and travelled back "home" occasionally, would all have been caught up in it.

Much to the surprise of my teachers, I did well in my CSEs, and was fortunate to be offered a much-sought-after job as a civil servant at the local office of the Department of Health and Social Security, where I worked interviewing people for welfare benefits. Later, I confounded my teachers' expectations even further by gaining 'O' Levels and 'A' Levels and continued to study part-time throughout my working life, eventually acquiring a degree in Psychology and Social Policy in the late 1980s.

Work opened up a whole new world for me. I was meeting new people, going to parties and making new friends, nearly all of whom were English. Apart from my family, the only Irish people I had contact with tended to be homeless men claiming the dole.

Through work, I met my husband to be, Charlie, from Manchester. He was studying electronics at college in Coventry and we hit it off straight away. We were married when I was nineteen, in 1972. A year later, Marianne, my daughter, was born.

Marianne was just a few months old when we moved into rural Leicestershire, away from Coventry and my parents into the heart of the English countryside. It seemed that now our family was no different from the other young families in the new housing estate on the edge of the village.

My transition into being English was now complete and over the next thirty years, apart from being aware of what was going on in Northern Ireland, I never gave my Irish identity another thought.

Chapter 25 - Resolutions

"Where did you get that accent?" a Dublin woman, slightly the worse for drink, demanded loudly. I blushed and stared at the ground. It was 2007, and Charlie and I were at a neighbour's party in Dunkineely; I had just told her that I was Irish, but had left Donegal when I was seven.

"Oh, but you sound so British," she trilled, mimicking my voice. I felt humiliated and cross. If our roles were reversed and she was in England, I would never have dreamt of commenting on her accent. She was being rude, but her words set me thinking. I don't remember ever making a conscious decision to adopt an English accent.

Speaking to a friend shortly after we came back to Ireland in 2006, I was surprised to learn that prejudice in England in the 1970s led her to tone down her Irish brogue. Had I done the same all those years ago, I wondered. Did I start to become English when I was bullied about my accent in the school playground. Was that when I made a subconscious decision to jettison my Irish voice and exchanged it for an English one? I wondered. Was that when I started to become English?

My last few hours in England were spent gazing through the window of our house, trying to work out whether or not I was making a grave mistake by returning to Ireland to live. It was a glorious summer's day and a familiar jumble of houses sat in front of me, behind sculpted lawns and brightly coloured borders. Suburbia nestling in the heart of England. Anyone would be happy to live there. So why was I leaving?

As I pondered that question, the phone rang. It was the solicitor, telling me that the money for the house had come through and we could proceed with the move. My heart skipped a beat. I turned to Charlie, my daughter and her partner, who were all glaring at me, concerned that there might be a further delay.

"Panic over, the money's through, it's all sorted," I said. "We're moving today, that's if the removal men ever turn up."

A collective sigh of relief flooded the room. We rushed together for a group hug. Another cup of tea, and the removal men appeared in a large truck outside. All at once, the place filled with bodies, bumping into each other, carrying boxes, moving furniture and cleaning up. By the time the final chair was squeezed in and the door of the van firmly shut, tempers were stretched to the limit and we all felt exhausted.

As the truck sped off, making for the ferry, I excused myself for one last journey around the only home I'd known for the past 27 years. Tears threatened as I meandered from room to room. The house had been our pride and joy: we had put so much of ourselves into it. When we first moved in, it had been an old gardener's cottage in need of renovation. Gradually, over the years, we had converted it to a four-bedroomed house, with an enormous light-filled dining room at the back, overlooking the garden.

I opened the patio door of the dining room and walked outside, breathing in the warm air. It tasted of an English summer. In front of me, elegant white phlox stood tall, jostling for space alongside blood-red dahlias and I could hear our laburnum tree swish faintly in the breeze. I sat down , unwilling for a moment to be parted from my beloved garden. Did I really want to leave all this?

Now that the time had come to leave, I was reminded of the old adage that you should never go back, but then quickly reassured myself that I could come back home again if I didn't like it. But where was home? I asked myself. Was it in England, where I'd spent most of my life, or is it where I was born: Ireland, the romantic land of rolling hills, of fiddlers and haunting tunes, of dark and smoky pubs. Was I just having last-minute jitters or had I left it too late to reclaim it, and make it my own? It was time to go.

After seven years, we are still in Donegal and I find my heart is hovering somewhere between Ireland and England. I am homesick for where I grew up, but at the same time, I am in love with Donegal. As I write, it is spring and the garden is awash with hundreds of forget-me-nots, framing the daffodils in the morning sunlight. Each year, as winter ends, I feel exactly the same: a surge of emotion as our garden comes to life.

As a gardener, I'm just a beginner, and for most of the year, I struggle to achieve a balance of colour and form to reflect the seasons but miraculously, I have accidentally managed to create a fabulous spring garden. It takes my breath away. It's hard to believe that just a few years ago, it was a quagmire of mud and rushes.

Eighteen months after we moved in, our friends in the Donegal Garden Society visited our emerging garden and pronounced it a great success. We had a grand evening when about thirty of our members donned Wellingtons, defied the midges, and gradually made their way around our acre of garden at the start of summer. All that weeding and pruning must have paid off. Later, as we enjoyed several bottles of wine together, there was much good advice given and accepted on future plans and projects.

These days my year is measured by what's in flower in the garden, watching the seasons unfold, wondering how my precious babies will fare in the Donegal weather or against an attack of greenfly. Maybe it's just about getting old, or maybe this preoccupation with the natural world is about my new life spent mainly out of doors.

Settling in Donegal has been a gentle process, as little by little, we have woven our way into the fabric of the community around us. My mental health problem lurks in the background, and sometimes I feel quite fragile, but for the most part I am well. My husband has been so understanding about my condition and supported me in any way he can, but I have found that the answer to my depression is to keep busy. Do things, don't spend my time gazing at my navel. And it works. I have joined a whole host of groups and they all keep me cheerful.

Most fun is the 'Page turners', a local book club, where we get together over wine and buns and fight about the merits of our read. I've also become a member of a writers' group. They're all saints and have patiently listened to several drafts of this memoir, offering endless encouragement and support. I have also become a member of the Donegal Abbey Singers and have relished every minute of it. When I'm not singing or reading, I go to a yoga class, and in the time I've left over, walk the highways and byways of the county. Thankfully, I seem to have achieved a good balance in my life and this has been helped by making many new wonderful friends, from around Dunkineely and beyond. Surprisingly, I have found that society in Ireland is not as hierarchical as in the UK, and people from all walks of life mix together here. Charlie and I count farmers, fishermen, teachers, musicians, tilers and writers, as our friends, a much more eclectic group than we had in England. So life is never dull.

Has the quality of our lives improved? For the most part it has. Our time is our own and we are free to pursue whatever projects we want. We have had a little part-time work, so our finances have not been too stretched. Ireland has been good to us. On the downside, I don't get to see my lovely daughters as often as I want. Sometimes I long for Jenny's cheery wit, as we enjoy some retail therapy together, or a companionable afternoon spent helping Marianne in her garden. Mostly I miss the intimacy of ordinary moments spent together, and the throwaway comments they make about tiny morsels of their lives.

For me the past seven years have flown by, but I was dismayed when the other day Marianne remarked, "But you've been away so long, Mum." It brought home to me, how much they miss us. If anything draws me back to England, it is my girls. I know it was our choice to move here, but I can't help wishing they were nearer.

What became of my first family, the ones who arrived in England in the 1950s to make a new life? Sadly, both my parents died young: my mother aged 59, my father just 66.

Not long before my mother's death, I came upon her in her kitchen, leaning over the sink, exhausted and near the end of her tether. I made her a cup of tea and we sat together by the gas fire, quietly reflecting on old times. I asked if she ever missed Ireland and longed to return. She thought for a moment, flashed a wistful smile and shook her head from side to side. "No, Ann. What is there for me back in Donegal? I'd miss the old mucky duck," her pet name for our home in Cambridge Street.

It's some consolation to me, that at least she lived to see my daughters and they have fond memories of playing hide-and-seek with her round the house.

My father passed away in 1987, just five years after Mum. Although he spent almost thirty years in England, he never truly left Donegal. It was as if he held himself in a bubble, cocooned from meaningful contact with those outside his Irish world. Mum once told me once that he always drank alone, that she felt pity for him, a solitary figure leaning on the bar with no friends to speak of. The only ones I ever knew him to have were Irish, people he had known from "home" before he came to Coventry. But he must at least have made a few connections for, after he died, his favourite drinking hole, a club for those working on the buses, christened a room in his honour. When Charlie and I found out, we paid it a visit. Sure enough, over the doorway was a sign, "Jim McFadden's Bar". An homage of sorts.

Are my brothers and sisters Irish or English? I'm not sure.

Pat has bought some land in Ireland and Carol has a holiday home here. Since we moved to Ireland, all my brothers have visited several times and Mary and Carol come at least twice a year. Although nobody has expressed a desire to live here, they all seem to have a strong affinity with the place and derive a great deal of satisfaction from family gatherings when they get an opportunity meet up with their Irish cousins.

They're definitely all Coventry kids, but somehow my coming back here has renewed the whole family's attachment to Donegal.

England was good to us. After an unpromising start at school, we ended up with five degrees, two MAs and a PhD, between us. It seems that whatever challenges we faced in our younger days, for the most part, we survived and flourished.

On a trip back to England to visit my daughters, I went with Marianne and Nic, her husband, to plant trees in an arboretum in Wolverhampton during national tree week. It was a sunny but freezing-cold February day and a small posse of us gathered around. Dressed in our Wellies and overcoats, wielding spades, we watched dutifully as we had a demonstration from one of the rangers on what to do. Suitably educated, we began a hectic couple of hours, digging holes, positioning our saplings in place and then securing them into the ground. When all was done, I stood chatting with the other volunteers, and it was then I realised that no-one had commented on my accent, or asked if I was here on holiday. In fact, I hadn't stood out at all. This is vastly different to Ireland, where from the moment I open my mouth, I'm defined as a foreigner. Sadly I realised that this will always be the case. In Ireland, I will always appear to be English.

One evening recently I watched a programme where celebrities trace their roots. The focus of this episode was a soap star, an Asian, who moved to Coventry from Kenya as a child. Like me, he was confused about his identity and wanted to trace his roots to give him a sense of where he belonged. Growing up, he'd often been rejected by his schoolmates as foreign, and so he'd developed a strong sense of being Indian. In the course of the programme, he travelled to Africa and India and although he found his ancestral home, in the end it seemed to him, his sense of identity was stretched across the three continents. I guess that's the fate of many young emigrants, a fracturing of their identities, so that they never truly feel at home in one place or the other. I've always envied people who are born and remain forever in their homeland. For example, my cousins in Loughfad, living in the spot their great grandfather farmed, must have given them a strong sense of where they belong.

When I was growing up and the question of nationality arose I would always declare myself Irish. But over the years, my feelings of identity changed and became more complex. When I first moved to England, it was simple: I was an Irish girl in a foreign country, but then as I began to settle in, my sense of who I am altered. Gradually I came to think of myself at least on the surface as English, especially as in the sixties it was fashionable and I was desperate to fit in. By the time I went to work, married and raised a family, my sense of Irishness had slipped away till it was almost forgotten. It was only much later, when I developed a mental health problem and I began to explore the possible causes of my problem, the issue of my identity resurfaced and I began to examine it.

When I moved to Ireland in 2006, it was to carve out a new life for myself, one that was laid back and stress free, but I also, deep down, I hoped to recapture my sense of being Irish. I knew that superficially I appeared to be English, but scratch beneath the surface, I told myself, and you will find an Irishwoman. Somehow I'd imagined that by returning to Ireland, I would automatically become Irish again. But now that I'm here, I find it's not that simple. Here, I am perceived as English, I speak with an English accent; I'm married to an Englishman. Although people have been kind, I'm very much treated as an outsider, not one of their own. Where does that leave me as I try to assimilate myself into the local environment? I'm not sure.

The legacy of the Troubles has meant that for many Irish people the old enemy, England, is still seen with some bitterness. There are occasional anti-English comments made by people around me, and for some reason, I bristle and spring to the defence of my old home. I don't know why I find it so annoying; I'm not even English. We have some friends who often argue that the problem in the North was not sectarian, but about class. Then I weigh in on the side of the Republicans and point to all the injustices the Catholic community endured over the years. I suppose the situation is like when your parents are divorced. You are constantly torn between them, and you try not to take sides, so end up constantly defending each one to the other.

Sadly, the feeling of loss I experienced when I left Donegal fifty-three years ago resurfaces from time to time, and coming back to Ireland has made little difference. Paradoxically being back in Ireland has not restored my sense of being Irish, but on the contrary, has made me feel more English.

If I'm honest, for most of the time, I've forgotten that sense of being part of the very earth of the place, the guts and the blood of it, that I had as a child. I now accept that the Ireland of my childhood is lost to me.

Except, that is, on a clear day, when the sun is high in the sky, when it's morning and I breathe in the sweet smell of the turf fire, or when I'm standing on the shore with my face held unapologetically to the wind. Then I feel a fleeting sense of its return, and I am home.

Lightning Source UK Ltd.
Milton Keynes UK
UKOW02f1032250215

246867UK00009B/102/P